Retire Rich

Retire Rich

The Boomer's Guide to Investing

Napoleon Robbins

Copyright © 2020 Douglas J Goodman
All Rights Reserved
ISBN- 9798618695886

Table of Contents

Part 1: Learning to Be a Superior Investor 1

1: Introduction 1
    Outline of Book and Who It's For 5
    The Three Character Traits of the Superior Investor 6

2: Risk 8
    1. There is a difference between a high or low risk investment and a good or bad investment. 9
    2. Risk is not the same as probability. 10
    3. Probability is nevertheless an approximation of risk in investing. 11
    4. Risk depends on context 13
    5. Risks must be managed rather than ignored 14
    6. At different times, markets are more or less risky 16

3: Retirement for Boomers 18
    Social Security & Medicare 20
    IRAs & 401(k)s 22
    Old Age Delusion 23

4: Risking Retirement 26
    Preliminary Steps 27
    Your Retirement Timeline 28
    Determine Your Necessary Spending During Retirement. 29
    Discretionary Spending 30
    Healthcare 30
    Income 31
    Withdrawing Your Money 32
    Reviewing and Updating Your Model 32
    Using Your Model to Test Scenarios 33
    Income Generation: The Encore Career 34
    Cutting Back on Discretionary Spending 35

5: D-I-Y 37
    My years at Madoff 37
    Financial Advisors 38
    Don't Buy & Hold Index Funds 40

6: Psychological Problems 44
    Emotions 44
    Fear 46
    Narcissism 47
    Psychological Problems in Investing 50

7: Macro Environment 52

    Predicting the Market 53
    Inflation 54
    Monetary Policy 54
    Interest Rates 55
    Economic Cycles 56
    Market Sentiment 57
    Politics 58
    Corruption 59
    Demographics 60

Part Two: What to Invest in Each Market 62

8: Read This 63
    Five Kinds of Markets 63
    Early Trending Up 64
    Late Trending Up 64
    Volatile 65
    Downturn 65
    All-weather Market 66
    Degree of Likelihood 66
    Don't Go Yet 67
    Diversification 67
    Cash 69
    How to Use the Following Chapters 70

9: Early Trending Up 71
    Transition to the new market 71
    Determining How Much and Where to Diversify 71
    Bonds 71
    Cash 72
    Exchange Traded Funds (ETFs) 73
    How to Buy an ETF 74
    Diversifying for Profits 74
    Small Cap ETF 75
    Investing in the World 75
    Sector Momentum Trends 75
    REITs 76
    Rebalancing 77

10: Late Trending Up 78
- Transition to the new market 78
- Fear of Missing Out 78
- Determining How Much and Where to Diversify 78
- Cash 79
- Exchange Traded Funds (ETFs) 79
- How to Buy an ETF 80
- High Dividend ETFs 81
- Diversifying for Profits 82
- Sector Momentum Trends 82
- Small-cap ETF 83
- Developed Market International Equity ETF 83
- Transitioning to Cash 84
- Transitioning to Bonds 85

11: Volatile Market 86
- Transition to the new market 86
- Determining How Much and Where to Diversify 87
- Bonds 87
- Exchange Traded Funds (ETFs) 88
- How to Buy an ETF 89
- Low Volatility ETFs 89
- Active funds 90
- Value Stocks 90
- Cash 92
- Rebalancing 93

12: Downturn 94
- Seven & Eleven Percent 96
- Bonds 98
- Cash 99
- Buying Back In 99
- Surviving a Long Recession 100

13: All-weather Market 102
- Fear of Missing Out 102
- Transition to the new market 102
- Diversification 103
- Exchange Traded Funds (ETFs) 103
- How to Buy an ETF 103
- High Dividend ETFs 104
- Sector Momentum Trends 105

  Bonds 106
  Commodities 107
  Cash 108
  Rebalancing 108

Part Three: Cheating, Murder & Getting the Hell Out 110

14: Getting Your Hands Dirty: Cheating and Murder 111
  Insider Trading 111
  Offshore Accounts 112
  Taxes 113
  Cheating on Your Wife 113
  How I Got Away with Murder 114

15: Retiring Abroad 117
  Choosing Your New Home 118
  Get the Hell Out 121

Part 1: Learning to Be a Superior Investor

1: Introduction

Why is that billionaire murderer writing a book? Why would the most famous (and infamous) investor of the 21st century decide to give away all his trade secrets? Why would the man who got away with it all now suddenly decide to give it away practically for free?

You've heard my name a thousand times. You think you know me. I get that all the time. You saw me on the cover of *Time* in 2009 proclaimed as a "Self-made Billionaire." You saw me on countless covers in 2018 walking into the courthouse in handcuffs. One year later, you saw me walking out of the courthouse in triumph, found not guilty of murdering my wife. Everyone's heard of my spectacular rise and fall. But you don't know the real story. I'm not saying that what really happened is more important than what everyone thinks happened. If everybody thinks I killed my wife, then I guess in a way, I did. And if everybody thinks that's a confession, then it is.

The upshot is that I can't trade anymore. I've been banned by the same crooked bastards that applauded me when I was making Wall Street rich. So, let's just say this book is my payback. I'm going to show you how to outsmart Wall Street and how to run rings around those Ivy League assholes. **You** living well will be my best revenge.

I'm going to tell you the secrets that the rich, greedy Yale MBAs don't want you to know. I'm going to tell you all those things that the Wall Street bastards will never tell you. I am going to tell you every smart move, every angle, every edge. You will win, and what's even better, *they* will lose.

More important than knowing how to get wealthy, I will teach you how to stay wealthy. After all this is what I used to do for a living before the SEC deemed me corrupt. Thirteen of the richest families in the world depended on me for all their financial advice, and they each paid me millions for the privilege. I give it to you for the price of this book. I just wish I could see their faces when you start taking all their money away.

I want you to forget everything you think you know about me. Everybody has the wrong idea. Everything that's been written about me is absurd. I'm not a "mad genius" as *Us Weekly* said. I'm not a "cold-blooded killer" which is what *National Enquirer* called me. I know what everybody thinks when I walk in the room. But that is not me. How easily the media can distort and destroy.

****

I came out of hiding recently to be interviewed by a *Wall Street Journal* reporter as a favor to the publisher, who had orchestrated favorable coverage for me during the worst of the press pile on. We agreed to meet in Zurich, since I had some business there anyway. The staff at the Baur au Lac all knew my real name and my current disguise. The reporter was brought over to my table in the lobby after she asked for my *nom de guerre*. She was young, Asian, professionally dressed.

The interview started badly. She asked about one of the two subjects we had agreed would not be asked: Where was I living now? When I refused to answer, she asked the second banned question: Had I killed my wife? From there, the interview went downhill.

Finally, she asked the question that every so-called expert with their brand-name education always asks me. "Do you really think you can beat the market?"

"Obviously I can," I answered curtly.

"How much longer do you think your luck can last?"

"Listen, honey," I jabbed my finger into her flat chest. "It's not about luck. You should write that down. NOT LUCK. I'll wait while you write it. N. O. T. space L. U. C. K."

"I don't need to write it down, Mr….er Sir." She'd forgotten my fake name. "I know it's not luck. I just thought that was a nicer word than fraud."

"Fraud? Well everyone's doing that, so it all evens out. It doesn't give you an edge. Let me tell you something about luck. You can't teach people luck. But I can teach anyone who wants to learn, how to consistently beat the market. I don't think you wrote that down. …NOT…LUCK." And that's when I first got the idea for this book.

"This interview is over," I said, ignoring her shocked look. I went up to my room and started plotting this book which would be my revenge on all those elite snobs who think that it must be luck or fraud every time an ordinary person becomes wealthy.

I'm going to tell you how I got rich and I'm going to teach you how to do the same.

A Real Financial Education

When I started out, I didn't have a book to teach me. But I got an excellent education at Harvard. I don't mean a useless MBA or a Doctor of Philosophy in Economics. That is nothing but bullshit book-learning. I wasn't at Harvard to get a degree. I was there to sell drugs. Being a drug dealer is the best possible preparation for being a superior investor. (BTW, It also helps when you want to get away with murder.)

I dealt mostly weed and coke, but usually had some heroin for the more *serious* students. Heroin and cocaine customers are insane and the dealer better have a touch of that himself if he wants to survive. And, obviously, the same can be said for any denizen of Wall Street. The first skill that the dealer has to cultivate is how to recognize the crazies. This is also the primary skill that you need to survive on Wall Street.

Pot smokers, on the other hand, are a discerning bunch. They wax eloquent about the quality of the high, and can take hours describing the smell of their favorite strain. In the marijuana market, the customer is king and the dealer better be good at reading the tastes and preferences of his market. Whether you're a drug dealer or an investor, you have to be able to read the market.

Also, the drug market is a freer market even than the stock market. It is not hampered by regulations. It isn't bound by laws. There are no fiduciary obligations. No legal contract is going to help you if you get screwed. No police will help if you get robbed. Its supply lines are global and unimpeded by any country's quotas or tariffs. If economists really wanted to understand a free market, they'd study drug dealers. It's what I studied and look where it got me.

After I got married, my wife convinced me that I'd never make enough money as a drug dealer. "With your skills, you'll make so much more on Wall Street. And then I'd be so much happier, and I would make you happy," she purred. Even though she turned out to be a low-class whore, she came from old money and had connections. She got me my first job on Wall Street with Bernie Madoff and I was with him until the Feds ruined a good thing. After that, I started my own hedge fund that catered only to the richest. I'd tell you their names, but they wouldn't mean anything to you. They pay a great deal of money to keep their names out of the paper.

Using street smarts and commonsense, I beat the assholes from Harvard, the bastards at Lehman's, the entitled twits at Goldman Saks. What would have happened to me if I had listened to those know-it-alls who told me that I needed an Ivy-league MBA? I guess I never would have outsmarted them in their own game, and maybe that's why they tried to sell that lie in the first place.

They think we're idiots, because we don't have a business degree from an ivy-league school, but we're smarter than they are. I know these chowderheads because I sold them drugs. They want their cocaine to look pure and white, just like they've seen on TV, and they buy in large lots, usually one stooge buying for the whole fraternity. They read Ayn Rand and take a macro-economics class and think they're intellectuals. They attend more parties than classes. They save the real thinking for how to get laid on the weekend without paying for it. They help each other cheat on exams and they make connections with the alumni that will benefit them later. And then they act like they made it on their own smarts. The only thing worse than a plain old idiot, is the self-satisfied, entitled, top-of-the-heap idiot.

We're not as stupid as they think. Our heads aren't full of grad school abstractions and theories about human behavior. Instead, we've lived a real life and developed some common sense. We don't have to know the formula for a standard deviation, we just have to learn how to use it. We don't have to do a linear regression; we just have to learn how to read a chart.

Long-term Capital Management was one of the great investment meltdowns of the modern age. With two Nobel-prize winners and countless professors, they were early users of mathematical investing. Unfortunately, the market isn't that good at math. When the market didn't follow the mathematical predictions of the eggheads, the firm plunged and burned, threatening to take Goldman Sachs, AIG, Berkshire Hathaway and half of Wall Street with them. Only a multi-billion dollar Fed intervention saved Wall Street. That's what happens when you put eggheads in charge of your money.

The fact is that they don't want us to know how to invest. They want us to be stupid. They like to think that they're the smart money and they want us to think so too.

Learning to be a Superior Investor

This book will teach you how investments, like the stock market, really work. I will show you how to avoid the average investor's mistakes. I'll teach you how to preserve your money with diversification and asset allocation. And how to add to your wealth with risk sensitive investments.

So many people are afraid of investing. They think the scam is on. The game is fixed. It's all chicanery or magic or insider trading. All of that is true to some degree. The market is fixed, where they are able to. There's plenty of chicanery and insider trading. But the fact is that the market is so chaotic and so overwhelming that those who think they can control it are the first to get screwed by it. Those who approach it with respect and self-discipline will learn how to win.

I'm not going to teach you how to become a master of the universe. I'm going to teach you how to become a superior investor. You won't "actualize your desires" by tuning into universal laws. Neither will you get the latest *hot stock*. There will be no *twelve-step plans*, no down-and-dirty, get-rich-quick schemes. If that's what you're looking for, there are plenty of authors who will take your money. If you are looking for *the secret*; if you plan on *thinking and growing rich*; if you are going to *manifest your desires*, then really your best bet is to keep buying lottery tickets until you make your million. What's the point of conservative investment strategies and diversified assets when you can just manifest your desires?

If you decide to go for the get-rich-quick scheme instead of working to become a superior investor, I don't blame you. You're an idiot, but it's not your fault. Our educational system has made you memorize the date of the Magna Carta and how to calculate the hypotenuse of a triangle, but they teach you nothing about investing. Have you ever had to figure a hypotenuse? Have you ever discussed the Magna Carta with your friends over a beer? But now your health, your comfort, your independence, perhaps your very life will depend on investing so that you have enough money to last the rest of your life.

Over your lifetime, you have seen company pensions turn into self-directed 401(k)s. You have been given complete control over your own retirement funding. You might have thought it a strange oversight that you've been given absolutely no instructions on how to intelligently invest, not even a quick course in the basics. If you're lucky, you've been taught to balance a checkbook, but most of us aren't even proficient at that. It's almost as if the lobbyists for the financial industry have set us up for easy pickings. Oh, wait a minute, it's not almost like that. It's exactly like that.

We live in a capitalist economy, but most people don't really know what capitalism is or even what capital is or how it differs from wealth. In fact, many people want to pretend that they're not capitalists. They like to imagine that they're way too ethical to care about money, which is, as everybody knows, the root of all evil. I've got news for you. It doesn't matter how many protests you attend, or how much money you give to beggars, or if you always vote the straight socialist ticket. You are a capitalist. You live in a capitalist economy. You depend on capitalism for your clothes, your housing, your daily bread. Protesters are just a niche market in the capitalist system. The money you give to beggars comes from and will be spent in the capitalist market. And even the most far-left political candidate is just promoting a different flavor of capitalism. (The irony is that the left's "socialism" is often a better version of capitalism than the right's lassez-faire).

Capital is money that works for you. It's wealth if it's sitting in your pocket, but it's capital when you put it in a bank and it draws interest or you invest it in a company and get a share of their earnings. Your retirement savings are capital, so you are a capitalist. You might as well get good at it. You've been taught how to work to make money, but you haven't been taught how to make money work for you. You've put a lot of thought into your career. You've read up on how to raise your children. Most of you have taken your time picking out this morning's clothes. But when it comes to investing, we just go with our guts. Unfortunately, most people's guts aren't very good investment advisors.

The Chinese have an especially nasty curse, "May you live in interesting times." Well guess what, you do. We've just been through the greatest recession in almost a century. New financial tools that nobody understands keep misfiring in unpredictable ways. Insider traders and market manipulators are getting richer. Economic irregularities and volatilities multiply. The Federal Reserve continues to experiment with unprecedented measures. We have a buffoon for president and clueless octogenarians for political leaders. Isn't this all *soooo* interesting?

Taking control of your investments is not some hypothetical possibility that we can contemplate in our leisure. It is a necessity. If you want long-term security, if you want the freedom that comes from having your money work for you, if you want an old-age of comfort and independence, you have to take control of your investments. If you don't the times will be more than interesting, they will be a terrifying horror-show.

Outline of Book and Who It's For

This book is divided into three parts. In the first part, I will teach you the basic concepts that you need to understand to be a superior investor. Here you will learn how to recognize which of the five kinds of market we are currently in. The second part is the meat and potatoes of the book. Once you know the kind of market, you will choose one of these chapters to guide you in your investments. Given the type of market, I will tell you exactly where to put your money and what dangers to look out for. Finally, the third section will show you how to stay wealthy.

There is no one-size-fits-all way to get wealthy. The advice for a twenty-four-year old kid just starting on his career is different than the advice for a recently widowed octogenarian. If you see a book that purports to give investment advice to everyone in general, you know that it's bullshit. This book teaches you how to RETIRE RICH. It says that right on the cover, so it must be true. Of course, everybody can get something out of these general ideas. Anyone who reads this will be a better investor, but it is written for the retired or those soon to be. The general ideas are true for anyone who wants to invest, but the practical application described in this book will be for the recently retired. That's right, Baby Boomers, this one's for you!

I should also admit that the audience I've had in mind as I write is predominantly male. I don't use the "he or she", "him or her", "dicks and cunts" inclusive crap that my editor keeps trying to slip into my writing. I think that any woman who is smart enough to take control of her own investments is also smart enough to get past the pronouns that I use. If not, you can always sue me for gender discrimination.

This book will teach you how to deal with uncertainty, how to overcome your psychological faults, how to analyze and interpret powerful economic forces and finally how to make enough money for you to retire comfortably no matter what political/economic/cultural catastrophes await us.

The Three Character Traits of the Superior Investor

This isn't just about money. It's about you. If you want to get and stay wealthy, you have to change. You have to become a very particular type of personality, the **superior investor**. Superior investors are different than **average-asshole investors**. Superior investors don't react out of fear. They face uncertainty with equanimity. They have self-discipline. They are winners. This book tells you how to change yourself. I will show you, step by step, how to become a superior investor. Here, already in the first chapter, I'm going to start. Before you learn about the macro-economy, or market volatility or risk assessment, you first have to work on developing these three traits.

Self-Discipline is the most important trait of the superior investor. You must have the discipline to follow your strategy despite the ups and downs of the market. If you abandon your strategy when it is down in order to switch to other investments that are up, you will always be selling low and buying high, the opposite of what you want. If you know you have no self-discipline, this book is useless. Instead of learning how to invest, first learn how to control yourself. Maybe join the Marines or Scientology. Try preparing for a marathon or losing fifty pounds. Or just follow through on every task, no matter how insignificant. See to it that you keep every promise, no matter how difficult. Work on that for a while and then come back to investing.

Flexibility is the second trait of the superior investor. The average-asshole investor sees self-discipline and flexibility as opposites. They think that you either stick with something come hell or high water or you are flexible. That is wrong. You can only be truly flexible when you have self-discipline. Investing requires that you adapt your strategies to changing circumstances, that you get rid of investments that aren't working, that you are able to change as quickly as the economic environment changes. The superior investor's changing strategies are responses to changing economic conditions. The average-asshole's changes are reactions to his own fear. You can only be sure that changed strategies are a response to changed circumstances instead of fear when you are confident in your self-discipline.

Patience is the third characteristic. I am going to teach you to make smart investments, but a smart investment is almost never the exactly right investment. Unless you are lucky enough to buy at precisely the bottom for a stock, you will be down at some point. Especially if you are investing to take advantage of long-term trends before others jump on them, you may have a long time-lag between your investment and making a profit. And if you are investing conservatively to preserve your capital, you must have the patience to sit out a bubble that everyone else is making money from. Patience is hard, but it's also your edge, your hidden advantage. Anybody who has lived through the ups and downs of an ordinary life knows more about patience than any Harvard MBA. The ivy-league brats are always thinking short term, while we know that what matters in life only unfolds slowly.

These three characteristics will serve you not only in investing, but in life. I think, for example, of my marriage. I had the self-discipline to not overreact when she cheated on me. I had the flexibility to consider all the ways that she could be taken care of. I had the patience, despite all her taunting, to wait until the moment was ripe. I only hope that your plans turn out as well as mine did.

2: Risk

Risk is the central idea upon which all investing is based. The primary goal of the superior investor is to get more return from their money with less risk.

The first question that a financial advisor will ask you is about your "**risk tolerance**." That is an *idiotic* question. It ranks right up there with asking someone their opinion of life on Jupiter. You can get long, detailed speculations from most people, but none of it really means anything.

The problem is that the financial advisor--with his Ivy-league education and the life experience of a Mayfly—doesn't mean the same thing by "risk" as what ordinary people mean. It's like someone asking if you prefer the color "blue" and forgetting to mention that by "blue" they mean "yellow." You may be able to explain the exact shade of "blue" that you prefer, but you're still going to end up wearing a lemon-color tuxedo to the wedding.

In their $100,000/year MBA classes, financial advisors are taught that risk is *volatility*. It's how much a price jumps around. This risk, they are taught, can be objectively and precisely measured. It is governed by statistics and predictable over the long run. According to them, you can tell which assets are high risk and which are low, and choose to invest in one or the other. And the market, in its infinite wisdom, will also know which investments are high risk and reward you more for your high-risk investments than for the low.

All of this is patently and unambiguously WRONG.

Here is the real definition of risk: "Many things *can* happen, but only one *will*. And that one might be bad."

Risk means knowing you might lose and doing it (or not doing it), anyway. Risk means being uncertain about the outcome. Risk means possibly losing your house; being unable to pay for medical care; outliving your money and being dependent on the "generosity" of some government agency. This is a risk that your young, well-heeled financial advisor can't comprehend.

But there is another thing that these penthouse-living, avocado-toast-eating, Chateau Margaux-drinking advisors don't know. Life is risky. Their career is not going to happen as they've planned. Their marriage won't be that stable. Their best friends will let them down. Their family won't always act like their family. They'll look back at their life as a string of broken promises and failed hopes. Shit happens and you deal with it. Life is risky. You deal with it.

Are we risk tolerant? Hell no! We are tired of taking risks. We'd like to never have to take another one. But here we are, on earth and not in heaven, so we have to. And it's really not that bad. There's even a little bit of earned dignity about it. But dignity or not, risk is our lot in life and so we grin and bear it.

All of life is risky, but the riskiest are those parts of life that lie in the future. Things happen in the future. You go out for a walk and the next thing you know you wake up on a traction bed, and a woman in scrubs is asking if you're really awake this time, and she's calling over a doctor who says "Well, I was wrong. I think he's going to make it." That's the risk you take by walking out your front door. You deal with it. And then the hospital sends you a bill for $200K. Have I said this before? You deal with it.

Investing is like life. It happens mostly in the future. All the outcomes and upshots, results and rewards, payoffs and punishments, consequences and compensations are in the future and therefore risky.

Markets are inherently risky. No matter what you've been told, they are not some efficient, rational machine. Markets are the accumulated wagers of millions of participants, some of whom are occasionally efficient, rational and predictable, but more often they are a brute mob swayed by fears and greed, dreams and nightmares, unrealistic hopes and all-too-realistic anxieties. When the market isn't being manipulated by predictable hucksters, irresistible fads and incorrigible corruption, its movements are, all too frequently, an unpredictable morass.

As long as the future is uncertain and bad things can happen, there will be risk. Understanding risk is the most important first step in being a superior investor. To save you all the research, I have formulated this understanding as six rules:

1. There is a difference between a high or low risk investment and a good or bad investment.

If the weatherman says there's an 80% chance of rain tomorrow and it doesn't rain, was he wrong, or right? Was that a good prediction? If you wear your galoshes to work and it doesn't rain, that was a bad prediction; if it does rain, it was a good prediction. But whether or not it rains has little to do with the accuracy of the weatherman's risk assessment. A single outcome tells you very little about the accuracy of the risk. Predictions are usually given in probabilities, but outcomes are always either 0% or 100%; they either happen or they don't. The <u>risk</u> of something happening is different from the actual <u>outcome</u>. Risky, uncertain, unpredictable outcomes happen all the time and many safe, predictable certainties never happen.

Let's say you decide to invest all your money in gold, as a safe and stable investment. The next day somebody announces the discovery of a new process to cheaply turn lead into gold. You made a bad investment, but not necessarily a risky one. Or maybe you invested it all in lead, in which case it was a good investment. But neither of these outcomes says anything about the riskiness. Risk has to be ascertained before we know the results, when the outcome is still uncertain, because that's what risk is, uncertainty about the outcome.

A risky investment is not the same as a bad investment. I once invested in special issue Qatari bonds. I was let in on the deal as a kind of a favor from one of my better clients. You usually needed two million to get in, but they let me in for a quarter of a share. A week later, the Qatari prince was assassinated by a servant who was then killed by a police guard, who then committed suicide. And when the prince's brother took over, all Qatari bonds were canceled. A very messy affair. The point is that what was a very low-risk investment turned into a bad investment.

"Take my wife," as Henny Youngman would say. Was she risky? Should I have gotten involved with her?

She came into the student center one day, sat down at the table where I usually sold my drugs. She was gorgeous: snub-nose, chiseled cheeks, freckles and blonde hair.

"You owe us money," she said.

"Who is us?" I asked.

"We take a cut of everything that gets dealt in Cambridge. We want our cut."

"Am I supposed to know you?"

"Shut up and listen," she said. "We don't mind a little side hustle if a brother needs some extra cash, but your dealing has become a regular thing and we want our cut." She glared daggers at me. "And I mean right now."

I looked over her outfit. A beige and pink dress with shoes that matched. Her makeup was perfect. Her manicure was immaculate.

"You're not really a tough guy," I said.

"Hand over your money and whatever drugs you have or you'll find out how tough I am."

I looked hard into her almond-brown eyes. "No," I said.

A smile lit her face. "Oh well, it was worth a try. I need some shit and I'm short on cash. But you're cute. Anything we can do to make a trade?" She reached under the table and started rubbing me in just the right place.

So I knew from the start that she was a drug-whore. But nobody's perfect and, heaven knows, I have my own blemishes. Of course, she was also a raging narcissist, but that can actually have its attractions. She undoubtedly would have killed me had I not…uh, prevented her. Maybe that's risky, but on the other hand, it made me the man I am. It was only knowing that she would kill me that spurred me to go beyond myself, to break through my own limitations and do what needed to be done. But the point here is that the risk and the outcome are two independent things. Even if you say, yes, my wife was risky, it still leaves you with 100% probability that she's dead. So who really was risky? Her or me?

2. Risk is not the same as probability.

Life has always been risky, but the concept of risk is recent. In other places and other times, people thought that gods or spirits, or the Great-Toad-in-the-sky determined their fate. If nothing else, there was Fortune, the Goddess that the down-and-out have always worshiped. There was no uncertainty, at least not up in the heavens. On earth, of course, things were different, but nobody paid that any mind, so long as they had the Gods to blame.

People first became aware of risk in games of chance sometime in the 16th century, but it was just an obscure mathematical study of repeatable, replicable events such as thrown dice, shuffled cards and roulette wheels. It hardly seemed to apply to the long-suffering variety of life.

Today we are told that everything, deep in its quantum world, is probability. What we thought were atoms are just waves of probability and reality itself is only probable. This demonstrates once again that no matter how irrelevant you thought those egghead theories were, they are far worse. Here in the real world, probability explains only a little of what happens. Nevertheless, the elite professors and academicians, making million-dollar salaries in their very un-ascetic ivory towers have created a vast array of statistical tools all based on the mathematics invented to predict the roll of dice. There is only one little problem: rolling dice (uniformly interchangeable events happening again and again) have little to do with the constantly changing environment of the market.

Probability only gives the sloppiest approximation of what actually happens in the market. Things regularly occur in the market that probability says should only happen once in a million years. For example, in 2007, Standard & Poor told us that the probability of a AAA mortgage bond going into default was 1 in 850. The next year 28% of them defaulted, over 200 times higher than probability predicted. Just recently, the market plummeted more than 5 standard deviations. That should only happen once every millennium. And then it did it again a week later. Instead of probability, the market is ruled by risk and uncertainty.

Probabilities are rational with outcomes forming predictable patterns over time. But uncertainty is irrational and unpredictable. It's the difference between Spock and Kirk. (See if this is too nerdy for you.) Spock always knows the probabilities and is therefore predictable. But Kirk is better for dealing with an alien enemy or an unknown force, because Kirk is intuitive and unpredictable. Therefore, Kirk would be the better investor. If that's too nerdy, then let's just say this is why computers haven't dominated investing. You can write an algorithm for probability but not for uncertainty.

An infamous and quickly hushed-up experiment demonstrated the difference between probability and uncertainty. Subjects in this experiment were instructed to play Russian roulette with realistic looking toy guns. The guns were cowboy-type six shooters, like you see in Westerns, and each was loaded with one small blank cartridge. After each squeeze of the trigger, they were to write down what they thought the probability was. It was hypothesized that how it was framed would affect the subjects' view of the probability, so half were told to write the probability of *winning* and half the probability of *losing*. Unfortunately, a student had brought his own gun into the lab (as you might guess, this was in Texas) and one of the students was killed.

Losing at Russian roulette is a probability. An idiot with a loaded gun is an uncertainty. The market is more like an idiot with a loaded gun.

3. Probability is nevertheless an approximation of risk in investing.

First, you must admit to yourself that there will always be uncertainty in investing. All kinds of unprecedented events happen with astounding frequency. New highs are followed by new lows; innovative financial technology blows up in interesting new ways; recently discovered butterflies flap new wings and there is an unpredictable pattern of economic chaos.

Probability oversimplifies the uncertainty. It distorts and perverts. Even after the outcome has occurred, probability gives only the most speculative of explanations. Probability can tell us something about investing, but what it tells us is only useful when we fully realize how distorted, oversimplified and subjective it is.

People like a good, hard number (this isn't just sexual innuendo). So, they focus on volatility. We can quantify an investment's past volatility, and probability can assign a precise number. The stock prices of small startups have jumped up and down quite a bit, so they are said to be riskier. Government bonds haven't jumped around, so they are safer. But studies have shown that this measure of risk depends on such things as the timeframe that the analyst chooses. If the investments are held for more than 20 years, the opposite is true, bonds are more volatile than stocks. In fact, economic history is full of complete and utter changes in risk. What was once boring and safe became a wild ride on a bucking bronc, and usually with no warning. Look at currency swings in 1997, oil in 1973, and real estate in 2008.

The market is not probable. It is not ruled by statistics. It is nothing more than the aggregate decisions of anonymous irrational humans trading back-and-forth with each other. Some are greedy liars and manipulators out to make a buck. Some are just part of the mob running after the latest momentum stock. People buy and sell for myriad reasons--some highly emotional, like divorce, death, medical emergencies--but mostly impulsive, foolish and bizarre reasons, and even a few rational ones, just to mix things up. Movements caused by the unrepeatable, unpredictable whims of human beings violate the assumptions required for statistical analysis. It is a miracle that probability and statistics can say anything at all about investing.

Nevertheless, for reasons I don't pretend to fully understand, probability does have something to say about the future of investing. I find it best to think of probability as if it were a religion. Let's call it the church of statistical probabilities. It works because people believe that it works. For example, if people are told that bonds are safe investments, the riskier speculators tend to stay away and therefore the investment is safer. Statistical analyses of the market are the sort of self-fulfilling prophesies that inspire all faiths. You should think of them like the moral rules of a religion. Usually followed but often broken and frequently in the most contrary and perverse way. You can expect the market to follow the statistical commandments to the same extent that you can expect Christians to refrain from coveting their neighbor's wife. But, as the Bingo Lady says, you have to know the rules if you want to gamble in the church. What she doesn't say is that you don't have to really believe in them.

It is useful to know some of the statistical measures, but it is also dangerous. The danger is not that these statistical measures don't work. No, quite the opposite. The danger is that they work up to the point where you've come to rely on them, and then they don't. And they usually fail at the very time that we need them most. Even worse, all the rules tend to fail at the same time because if one statistical probability or moral rule is broken, you can expect people to throw up their hands, declare the sky is falling and precede to break other rules. The danger of believing in probability is that it can obscure the real risk of uncertainty.

The superior investor must be able to evaluate the amount of risk taken in trying to achieve the desired return. Risk cannot be reduced to an exact probability based upon past volatility. With investing, risk always includes an essentially unpredictable uncertainty. Statistics are useful if we keep that uncertainty in mind. They are a good starting point for evaluating our risk. They are dangerous if we think they measure something real.

4. Risk depends on context

Remember, risk means that many things can happen, but only one will, and that one might be bad. With this definition in mind, it is clear that risk can't be a precise, objective probability, but is instead dependent on the context. If a young, millionaire financial advisor stands to lose $20,000 in an investment, that's hardly a risk. Even if they are down to their last million, they can just "borrow" more from Daddy. But for middle-class retired people, losing $20,000 in an investment is risky indeed.

Even if we just look at volatility, the more money you have, the easier it is to ride out those periods when the investment goes down. If you only have $20,000 and your investment goes down more than that, you won't have any money invested when the market goes back up. But people with a couple million invested will see their investment go up or down by $20,000 on almost a daily basis. For young millionaires, volatility is just an opportunity to buy when the market is low and sell at the high. For a retired person, it might mean being unable to pay for the necessities during the down times or, at the very least, being forced to sell when the market is down and endangering future necessities. When you're retired, you only have one portfolio to live on, no Daddy to borrow from, and one shot at making it last.

For the retired person, there are more risks than simply making a bad investment. There's the risk of runaway inflation, or the risk of artificially suppressed interest rates. And these risks are increased if we don't make investments. There are even some risks that we're happy to take, although they may be catastrophic in the end. For example, the risk of outliving our money. Investing is always risky, but for most, not investing is even riskier.

Before you can evaluate the risk of the investment, you must first evaluate your own ability to take risk. I don't mean what the financial advisors call your "risk tolerance." Screw that. You take risks when you have to and avoid them when you can. I mean your ability to withstand a risk if it goes bad.

The risk of a particular investment is more dependent on your circumstances than it is on the volatility of the thing you're investing in. Your ability to take risk can be boiled down to three factors. The first is how long before you'll need ready cash. This includes not only predictable near-term cash requirements, but also how much you have on hand for unanticipated emergencies. The more money you have on hand, the less the risk of investing. The second factor is the predictability of continuing income. For example, if you have social security, a pension, rent income, etc. then your risk of investing is less. Finally, there is your ability to implement a plan B. If in an unanticipated emergency or a catastrophic loss, you have an option, then you have less risk. For example, if you have a second home that you could sell, or could get a part-time job or are able to drastically cut back on your spending, you have less risk.

Context matters. My entire career has been risky, but the type of risk changed when I went from dealing drugs to Wall Street. The probability of losing your life in a drug deal may be the same as the probability of losing money in an investment deal, but I can tell you that I felt a cold, clammy hand tighten around my balls every time I went into a drug deal, and I felt calm, cool and collected in every financial deal, even in those where I knew I would probably lose a lot of money.

One of my investing clients was an extreme skier. He loved the thrill of long, steep slopes that nobody else dared to go down and where one mistake could leave you dead or a quadriplegic. But when it came to investing, he only wanted the safest bonds. Some might call his sport one of the riskiest, but he just didn't see it that way. "It's all about your mental state," he told me. What was risky to another person was not to him and vice versa. What would his answer mean if he were asked by his financial advisor, "How much risk are you comfortable taking?"

Anybody who has lived long enough in the real world, knows that risk depends on the context. This is why you are the person who is best positioned to determine what is or is not a risky investment. You know your own context (rich or poor; young or old; smart or stupid; anxious or calm, etc.). You can't really trust those trust-fund babies who think they can advise other people how to deal with risk. Even if one happens to have your interests at heart (see Chapter Five for how likely that is), they wouldn't have your context.

5. Risks must be managed rather than ignored

Risk is inherent to investing. But investing risks are not simply a matter of luck. Unlike luck, an investor's risks can be managed. The risks in markets are much more like the risks in poker or horse racing than dice or roulette. In the former, there is some skill involved, especially the skill of knowing what kind of mistaken bets the other players tend to make. With dice and roulette, it's just a matter of luck and probability.

There is an aspect of investing that makes it different from any kind of gambling. Gambling, whether dice, cards or horse racing, is a zero-sum game. For every winner (usually the house), there is always a loser (usually you). But investing represents a piece of a company that is liable to grow. Economies grow, productivity grows, innovations appear and there is every chance that the value of the stocks you invest in will grow. Investments can create new wealth. Gambling just moves wealth around.

The word "risk" comes from the Medieval French, *risquer*, meaning to dare. Daring is part of modern life, from such large-scale events as military provocations, technological perils, and environmental threats to the small-scale, such as health care decisions and marriages (as I found out to my chagrin!).

Because investing deals with the future, it's always risky. You're always daring the fates. There's always an element of uncertainty that is completely unpredictable. The chance that we'll lose is always there as a cold, hard reality.

Investing risks must be managed rather than avoided. Managing risk means anticipating what plausible bad things can happen and considering how you'll deal with these bad results.

The first step in managing risk is to distinguish those risks that can be avoided from those that can't. There's a level of uncertainty in all investments that can't be avoided, minimized or even predicted. Stocks undergo random gyrations, currencies hit inexplicable spikes and billions of dollars are lost and recovered in a matter of minutes. For example, on May 6, 2010 the stock market lost over a trillion dollar in less than a half hour and recovered most of it 15 minutes later. Nobody predicted this "flash crash" and the experts still disagree over the cause of it.

Other risks can be avoided or minimized. For example, if you already have enough money to last a lifetime, you can completely avoid stock market risks and expose yourself only to the risk that Western civilization will collapse. Those who need to generate some income during retirement must learn to minimize and manage the stock market's necessary risks.

The key to risk management is to minimize the impact from risks over which you have no control and to maximize the areas where you have some control over the results. Most of us are already familiar with this idea in that we've decided to pay for house and car insurance to minimize the consequences of our car getting totaled by an uninsured driver or our house getting burned down in a forest fire. Insurance is how we manage our risks. It doesn't eradicate risk. We hope we don't "win" the big payout from the insurance company and are happy to lose the bet we make every month with our premium payments.

Although people are happy to lose money with insurance, the same isn't true of investing. Investors expect to be paid for their risk. Investing can be defined as bearing risk in return for the possibility of profit. Superior investors make sure that they have the best chance of making a profit for the amount of risk that they take. The goal of the superior investor is to maximize the profit while minimizing the risk.

People who don't know how to manage risk end up ignoring it. We'll talk about this more in Chapter Six Psychological Problems, but for now let me briefly say that our minds were not built to analyze risk and therefore one must learn, usually through painful experience, how to fully accept the possibility of loss. Otherwise, investors only contemplate their risk in the most abstract way and don't consider what it would really mean to completely lose this bet. Worse, to avoid the thought of losing, they convince themselves that they cannot lose. This is the absolute worst way to manage risk.

The best way to manage risk is to try to make sure that your return is commensurate with your risk. We risk investing, but we expect to be paid for it, and as much as possible. The average-asshole investor looks only at the return, the possibility of winning. The superior investor looks also at the risk, the possibility of losing. And he makes sure that he gets the best return for the risk.

There are some who will tell you that the return is always commensurate with the risk. They think that the omnipotent & omniscient market knows the amount of risk and always pays a fair return. They'll show you a risk/return chart suggesting a direct relation between the two. (See figure 1)

That widely-used chart is a complete fabrication and doesn't rest on any actual data. The relation shown in this chart is not between risk and return, but between investors' perceived risk and return. The superior investor does not confuse these two. The perceived risk is a collection of others' whims and fancies, but the real risk is grounded in your context (see Rule Four). Superior investing takes advantage of those times when the real risk is less than the perceived risk and avoids those times when the real risk is more than the perceived risk. Never think that something is less risky just because the return is lower or that something is riskier just because of a higher return. You have to make your own judgment about the risk because only you understand your own context.

Since the superior investor learns from his past judgements, he gets better at evaluating the risk. More and more, he is correct in his assessments and the results are positive. Sometimes the market will even cooperate, and for a time, it will act predictably and, one might even say, rationally. In such good times, it's easy to forget about risk management and sink into the psychological error that we *must* be right. That's how superior investors become average-asshole investors.

While most investors try to avoid risk, there are those who love the thrill. That too must be managed. You see a lot of that among drug users. Quite apart from the effect of the drug, risk itself can be addictive.

My wife loved risk. She was always ripping open my pants and giving me head in risky places. I'm not into sex in public places, but I did it to make her happy. I think she liked to see my nostrils flare, my eyes dart about, the thrill tingle through me as I came as fast as I could before we got caught. She'd take my dick out her mouth and say, "Relax will you." But I never could. It was just a risk that I had to manage.

6. At different times, markets are more or less risky

The tendency to pursue risk is not confined to individuals. It is one of the mob movements that can affect an entire market.

When the market is acting rationally, people demand more return for more risk. However, during bull markets, especially long ones, people start to forget that risk is dangerous and they no longer demand a premium to compensate for the risk. People think that since higher risk promises higher returns, the more risk the better. This is the riskiest time for the superior investor.

When investors are afraid of risk, they demand a high premium for it. A market that pays high premiums for risk is a less risky market. When investors are unafraid of risk, the market pays low premiums for it and is therefore riskier. This is called the perversity of risk.

When others are unafraid of risk, the superior investor will avoid risky investments because the market will not adequately compensate him for the risk he takes. This is not an easy rule to follow. The mob will be plowing all their money into the riskiest investments which will go up as a result. The superior investor must realize that even though he's missing out on the fabulous altitude of high-flying stocks, he's also missing out on taking risks for which he is poorly compensated.

This is also true for "chasing returns." When the fed sets interest rates low, some investors will move to ever more risky bonds, such as junk bonds, to get the desired return. However, the Fed decision also artificially suppresses the return on junk bonds, so the investor is getting paid less for taking the risk. The investor may have found the yield they want, but they end up taking much more risk. When investors are willing to take less of a premium for such risky bets as junk bonds, that is the worst time for the superior investor to be in them.

Retire Rich

We take risks in our life, in our marriage, in our career and in our retirement. Risk cannot be avoided. Risk should not be ignored. The goal of the superior investor is to have the maximum return for the minimum risk. But we cannot fall into the delusion that it is a hard, measurable quantity, that it is a probability. The superior investor starts from the probability of volatility, but judges the risk by his own circumstances. He begins by carefully considering what would happen if he were wrong. If he cannot afford to lose on that investment, then the risk is high, no matter what the probability suggests. He must also consider the market. If investors are generally risk averse, the risk to the superior investor is lower and vice versa. The superior investor evaluates the risk in advance and learns from his failures.

3: Retirement for Boomers

For most of us, the chief purpose of risk and investing is to retire on the money we've made. After slaving and saving for so many years, you're given the gift of freedom—from work schedules, from deadlines, from getting up every god-damned morning and fighting the commute only to turn around every night to face an even worse commute home. And, as an added bonus, you won't need as much money. You don't have to pay as much in gas or car expenses. You don't need the fancy work clothes and best of all, you don't have to squirrel away some of your money every month for your retirement.

If that's your view of retirement, I have some bad news for you. The freedom of retirement means that you have to set your own schedule, routines, goals and rules. And you must have the self-discipline to stick to them. Otherwise, you sit in front of the TV and watch Fox News all day. As far as spending less money, remember that you once had such long days at work where you had little time to spend money. Well, now you have plenty of time to do things and don't you think that a lot of what you do will cost money?

According to your financial advisor, retirement is the time to move your money into risk-free investments, hunker down and enjoy the good life. What your head-up-his-ass advisor won't tell you is that there are no risk-free investments because we don't know what will happen in the future. As we discussed in the previous chapter, risk cannot be avoided, it can only be managed. Pretending that there are risk-free investments is the worst possible way to manage risk.

Retirement investing, like all investing, involves risk since it deals with the future. I am going to tell you step-by-step how to manage that risk, but let's start with the greatest financial risk to your retirement, the risk that Social Security and Medicare will disappear or be drastically cut back.

My wife, God rest her soul (or whatever she had in place of a soul), believed that the whole idea of retirement is a scam. "Promising retirement is how we keep the peons working at meaningless jobs. We promise them that someday they won't have to slave and sacrifice. They'll be free to do what they want. Someday, we promise, they'll be like us. But you know what, they never will."

She's right, of course. Some cultures promise the poor a seat in heaven, we promise them a blissful retirement. For a poor person, the chance of either of those is about the same.

We have a good scam and want to keep it going. But we aren't doing a very good job. Nothing that will happen in the future is set in stone, but the risk of losing Social Security, and especially Medicare; or having them drastically cut, is increasing. The risk is going up and we need to be prepared. Like any other risk, it needs to managed rather than ignored.

Unless you're an idiot, you probably already know all this. Anyone can see that we are increasingly being left to our own resources to deal with problems that are caused by the society we live in. If technology eliminates the job for which you trained and in which you have years of expertise, tough luck, you're on your own. If globalization means that your occupation can be outsourced for half the price, you're on your own. If the feds make it hard for you to get a new job because they want to keep inflation down, you're on your own. If the FDA and AMA push addictive drugs and in your jobless despair, you develop some expensive new habits, you're on your own. Pretty much anything bad happens and you're on your own. (On the other hand, if anything good happens, like winning the lottery, the government will be sure to take their cut.)

This is no less true of retirement. If your retirement is trashed because Congress can't do its job of enacting reasonable compromises, you're on your own.

You see them out on the street corners with signs "Will Work. Need Food. God Bless." They come up to you outside grocery stores. They clean your windshield on busy streets. They congregate outside the Salvation Army. They collapse on doorsteps and scramble into dumpsters. Many are about your age. You don't know if you should feel fear or empathy or some wild mixture of the two.

Everyone knows someone once middle class, now slipping into bankruptcy. Someone who keeps borrowing money, never quite able to pay it back. Someone in dire straits through no fault of their own. They didn't commit any crimes. They weren't alcoholics. They didn't gamble their money away. It's just the ups and downs of life when you have nobody in your corner. The grey-haired pizza delivery man. The Walmart greeter. The arthritic waitress. The elderly laundromat attendant. Once they dreamed of retiring to the Bahamas. Now they just hope they can make it through one more day, one more humiliation.

Because I'm famous, I hear from these people all the time. They write me. They want my help. Anything I can spare. Any advice. Any money. If I know them from before I was rich, I help where I can. But there's only so much an individual can do. One person can't cure the ills of society. So don't write me asking for money.

The current situation can't continue and it's getting worse. The national debt is exploding. There are more and more people retiring. More and more of them are poor. There are more and more expensive prescriptions, medical procedures, life-saving devices. Social Security and Medicare cost more and more, and there are fewer and fewer young workers to pay for it. We are facing a catastrophe that our political leaders seem incapable of handling or even acknowledging. It's foolish to simply ignore this and pretend that Social Security and Medicare will be there for us when we need it.

The first thing that you must realize is that retirement is not some God-given, universal right. Most people throughout most of history didn't retire. They worked until they couldn't, and then their kids took care of them, one way or another (e.g. seating them outside, surrounded by their most cherished possessions and leaving them to freeze to death). Retirement is a 20th century creation. It never existed in previous centuries and it very well may not survive much longer in this one.

The time when our corporate employers will take care of us from the start of our career to the end of our life is over. The time when you took care of your parents and your children will take care of you is over. You can't rely on your job. You can't rely on your family. You can't rely on government programs. The retirement that you were promised will be gone. No law-abiding, tax-paying, church-tithing life will sustain you. No relationship will protect you. No institution will shelter you. This isn't pessimism; this is reality.

Social Security & Medicare

As the reality hits them, most people in our generation will rear up on their hind legs and cry out, "We've been lied to. We've been cheated. We earned our retirement. We deserve it." Well, the fact of the matter is that we didn't earn it. Previous generations fought for it and we simply inherited it. And we've handled it badly. People who are given a working, sustaining retirement system and treat it like a piggy bank that they can raid at their whim can't really say that they deserve it.

Some people will say that they've put money into the government's Social Security all their life and they just want the money back that they've invested. Some experts might call this an understandable misconception. I call it willful idiocy. Social Security was never like a pension. You don't put in your money when you're young and take it out when you're old. It doesn't work that way and it never has. Social Security and Medicare have always been an immediate transfer from current workers to current beneficiaries. Your parents and grandparents thank you very much for the money, because that's where it went. It hasn't been saved up for your retirement. Your retirement depends on the generosity of current workers. And a lot of those workers, seeing the greed and mismanagement of the boomer generation, aren't really in a very generous mood.

The first pensions were instituted because the soldiers of the Roman Empire were marching into Rome laden with foreign booty and bristling with weapons. After a few military insurrections demanding a cut, Rome decided it was best to pay them a pension and give them some land scattered about the provinces far from Rome. After the American revolution and our civil war, American leaders made the same calculation. Pensions were not something that long-suffering workers deserved. It was something that armed insurrectionists demanded. It wasn't social justice, it was threats and fear.

The Social Security program was also driven by fear. It was one of the many experiments that FDR tried during the Great Depression to resuscitate a failed American economy. Before Social Security, over half of senior citizens lived in poverty. Today it is less than 10%. Social Security worked so well that politicians did the math and decided to keep it going into perpetuity. After all, for every person drawing money out of Social Security, there were 42 workers putting money in. And that one person getting Social Security didn't get it for very many years. He didn't start drawing on it until he was 65 and the average life expectancy was 62.

But the math has changed, today there are only three workers for every retired person, and soon it will be closer to two. And the average number of years that retirees draw on Social Security and Medicare is over 30. For the past 10 years, Social Security has paid out more than it takes in and experts believe the Social Security Trust Fund will be depleted by 2034. Medicare will go broke even earlier in 2026. Now you might be one of those who doesn't believe in math. Maybe you're expecting some great scientific breakthrough where subtraction starts to act like addition and all the money for your Social Security and Medicare are returned. Best of luck with that.

Realistically, you're going to live a long time, possibly longer than any savings could last. Realistically, your health will get worse. You may have counted on Social Security and Medicare. That may not be the most realistic plan.

If retirees' longevity continues to rise and the cost of new medications and medical procedures continues to increase, then there are really only two possible outcomes. Either everyone's taxes will go precipitously up, or we will live in a country of rampant elderly homelessness, untreated disease, premature deaths and social unrest.

The problem is that raising taxes can only work up to a point. It has never been that successful in bringing in more income, and high taxes are even less likely to work today. Those with the most money to contribute are the most mobile in this globalized world. It's easy for them to hide their money in offshore accounts or to take up citizenship in a low tax country. In addition, the rich will have every economic incentive to hire lobbyists to sneak loopholes into any tax bills and then lawyers and accountants to help them exploit the loopholes. Doesn't that already sound familiar? Now just imagine the special loopholes that will be exploited if taxes go up. The politicians may say that they're raising taxes on everyone, but you can bet that the brunt of it will fall on the young middle-class.

Let's look at the world from the viewpoint of the young middle-class workers who we count on to pay for our retirement. When this younger generation were investing in their education, politicians refused to subsidize their education by funding affordable state universities like they did for the baby boomers. Instead, the government just made it easier to borrow money, so that they came out of college with unprecedented amounts of debt. As they were beginning their careers, they were hit with a Great Recession caused by the lies, corruption and greed of the Boomers. While the Boomers had seen their home values rise throughout most of their life, this generation's young people have seen them stagnate. But that's not so bad, since the young are one-third less likely to be able to afford their own house. Their salaries have languished while the Boomer CEOs and stockholders' income has skyrocketed. And then just to put a cherry on it, the Boomers gave themselves a big tax cut in 2018 which, of course, the next generation will be expected to pay for. Most of the younger generation do not believe that Social Security and Medicare will be there for them, and 80% of them are unable to set any money aside for their own retirement. Can we really expect them to double their taxes in order to pay for our botched retirement?

But don't they love us? Won't they take care of us? A recent study at Yale University looked at that very question. Young subjects were given a leaflet showing how much each of them would have to pay in order for senior citizens to have a comfortable retirement. They were then taken into a darkened room with a two-way mirror where they could see an elderly person in the next room strapped to a chair. The subjects were told that they could push a button that would administer an electric shock, and they were given a contract that promised them anonymity and freed them from any liability. After a few tentative pushes, most of the subjects quit using the button.

The researchers decided to run the experiment again because they suspected that the subjects knew that the elderly person was only an actor who pretended to be shocked. When they replaced the actors with real elderly people and hooked up actual electrical shocks, the subjects administered so many shocks that in many cases, the researchers had to rush into the room and restrain them. One of the researchers, who was also elderly, was beaten unconscious by a young subject who then proceeded to administer enough shocks to the elderly woman to require hospitalization. The researcher found that the gender and race of the elderly person made no difference and that subliminal images of homeless old people only increased their propensity to administer shocks (as did subliminal images of President Trump and Nancy Pelosi, especially together).

Believe what you will about the future, but any rational person would say that the risk of losing Social Security and Medicare needs to be planned for and managed.

The first step in managing the risk of losing Social Security and Medicare is accepting that you're on your own. You didn't cause the impending crisis. At least not you as an individual. Your society, your culture, your institutions, your generation caused this, nevertheless each individual is left to deal with it as best you can.

Despite the facts, many retirement books would shame you into thinking that you had caused the crisis. You just didn't save enough. You didn't invest correctly. You didn't think ahead. When you should have been saving for your retirement, you were frivolously paying for your kids' college. When you should have been figuring out the best investments, you were wasting your time earning a paycheck. You should have known that Social Security and Medicare wouldn't be there for you, but you stupidly accepted your nation's promise that it would. Let's just admit that we were all idiots and move on. The point is not, "Who can we blame?", the point is "What do we do next?"

IRAs & 401(k)s

With the collapse of pensions, with the threat to Social Security, most Americans are left with a do-it-yourself system of 401(k)s and IRAs for their retirement income. The primary purpose of this system is to shift responsibility for a failing retirement system from society to the individual. It can have the secondary effect of funding your retirement, but that wasn't the primary purpose and it's not easy and often fails.

The 401(k) was not a planned policy devised by our wise legislatures to deal with the pressing social problem of retirement. An accountant noticed a little quirk embedded in the 1978 tax code that allowed workers to set aside a portion of their paycheck into a dedicated account. The accountant said, "Let's pretend that this account is tax deductible." The IRS, encouraged by financial industry lobbyists, said, "Sure! Why not!" And so, a new kind of retirement account, the 401(k), was born. At first it was only used by overpaid executives of big corporation, but eventually the executives realized how much money they could save if they got rid of pensions for their workers and replaced them with 401(k)s. Today, there are few pensions left.

Of course, the 401(k) has been great, at least for investment firms, mutual fund companies, hedge funds, private equity funds and human resource departments. For those hoping to fund their retirement, not so great.

With pensions, you knew you were good for however long you lived. If the employer's benefit manager miscalculates and their employees live longer than anticipated, the company will pay for it. With the 401(k), if the benefit manager (you) miscalculates and the employee (again, you) lives longer than anticipated, then the individual (you, for the third time) will pay for it. And by pay for it, I mean dying in poverty.

The primary disadvantage of 401(k)s and especially IRAs is that you decide how the money is invested. Unfortunately, most of us are not very good at making such decisions. The point of this book is to turn that disadvantage into an advantage. This book will teach you how to make the best decision about investing the money that you will need to cover the shortfall when those lying bastards pull the rug out from under the Social Security and Medicare benefits that you've been counting on.

Old Age Delusion

Few people are prepared for the increasing risk of losing Social Security and Medicare. Indeed, few are prepared for getting old and sick even with Social Security and Medicare. There are two reasons for this: (1) We are deluding ourselves; and (2) politicians and marketers are profiting off the delusion.

Retiring Baby Boomers are planning to spend more money in their retirement by traveling around the world, continuing to live in an expensive family home and enjoying the good and expensive things in life. They are also planning on living longer. Many people would think that it is unreasonable to expect to spend more, live longer and not expect to go through your retirement savings, but the Baby Boomers have a plan to deal with that. They will save money by not ever getting old and sick.

Most Boomers are in the early years of their old age. They are still in reasonably good health with little cognitive decline and few debilitating diseases. They see no reason why this shouldn't continue until sometime in their late 90s when, after a vigorous and prolonged bout of lovemaking, they roll over and gently die in their sleep.

Baby Boomers have always been full of confidence. Their entire life has been a time of economic upward mobility, increased education, an expanding job market and multiplying choices. They watched their grandparents retire to relaxed leisure and they expect their retirement to be even better. A study of history or even a glance at the ongoing trends might argue that this can't last forever. But to even think that goes against the Boomers' philosophy of positive thinking. Never give up, just try harder. Never get old, just try harder. Just Do It!

Boomers have come to believe that their old age will be radically different from any other old age in history. Perhaps for a few of those with the right genes, lifelong devotion to good health and abnormal good luck, it will. But the rest of us can expect a period of increasing frailty leading to cognitive impairments, disability and a slow-motion death requiring long term care. It may come later than previous generations and it may last a longer time, but neither of these aspects of the new old age are going to be very good for our financial health.

The Boomers have always believed in endless reinventions. They've experimented with various sexual partners, dabbled in different careers, divorced and started again with whole new families. The useful message that you can change, has morphed into the absurd message that you can do anything as long as you keep thinking positive thoughts. They've come to believe that they can recreate the biology of old age just by "thinking young" and eating the right macroketopaleomediterraneanhearthealthypescovegetarian diet.

Boomers won't even refer to themselves as old or getting older and no marketer hoping to get their business would dare use the "O" word. Age is no longer a biological fact, it is "just a number." Going online (http://www.biological-age.com/), Boomers can put in their pretend healthy diet and their fantasy exercise regime and get their "real" age, which gets younger every time they do it. They can extend their lives with the appropriate "lifestyle" and the help of memory computer games, daily antioxidants and the usual promises of pharmaceutical companies. But even if true, that only puts off the disabilities of old age. Boomers are, in fact, even more likely than previous generations to require expensive long-term care simply because they are living longer. They may be able to postpone it, but Boomers are going to have to face that they cannot bend old age to their will.

Such delusions are far from harmless either for the individual or for society. Our resulting lack of action makes all of these problems worse and will require more draconian solutions. If we are going to manage the risk of growing old, frail and disabled, and of losing the Social Security and Medicare that we counted on to sustain us, the first thing we must do is to acknowledge that these risks are real.

We cannot expect any help from society. The disabilities of old age hit those that are over 85 the hardest. In ten years, they will be the fastest growing part of our population. Our plan for dealing with that demographic tidal wave is to try not to think about it as we watch the independent, healthy and cheerful gray-haired actors on our TV screens who enjoy life and don't seem to ever need anyone's help. None of them are in a wheelchair, only those surrounded by loving families have dementia, none are eating their meals from a tin can. Inundated by such pleasant images, why would anyone want to face the difficult choices necessary to prepare for the future?

You only need to look at the uproar over Obamacare "death panels" to see the depth of the delusion and its harm. One-quarter of Medicare spending occurs in the last year of life. One third of that is in the last month. Many elderly people do not want the expensive, invasive care required to extend their comatose lives for a few more days, but they get it anyway because they haven't thought ahead to make the decisions that will allow them to die a peaceful death. Doctors have estimated that end-of-life discussions could save Medicare $75 million a year. So, Obamacare provided subsidized, voluntary consultations with a physician to discuss the individual's wishes for their end-of-life care. This proposal, which would have both saved money and honored the person's wishes, was labeled a "death panel" and removed from the bill. Apparently, even talking about our end-of-life care challenges our delusions, and that will not be allowed.

Or look at most people's plan to pay for their long-term care. A recent poll reported that over half of Americans expect Medicare to pony up for their long-term care. That would be a good plan except that Medicare doesn't pay for long-term care. And there is next to zero chance that will be changed in the future, since Medicare is already going broke as it is. To put it in a nutshell, most people's plan for their own care when they are at their most vulnerable is nothing but a delusion.

The myth of a problem-free old age and the fact of our increasingly divisive politics means that it is less and less likely that we will take any of the difficult steps to preserve Social Security and Medicare. Fidelity Investments estimated that a healthy couple who retired in 2017 would need an average of $275,000 for health care costs. That is with today's Medicare coverage. You should consider how you would handle things if Medicare is drastically cut and you have less Social Security for income.

Retire Rich

I had to admire the way that my wife took care of her mother's retirement. She put her in a nursing home as soon as she became a nuisance and slipped some extra barbiturates into her vodka when she started complaining too much. It was a peaceful, painless death. I thought of this when it became time to take care of my wife. I didn't really care if it was painless, but peaceful doesn't disturb the neighbors and gives you time to hide any incriminating evidence. Personally, I wouldn't recommend this for everyone. But it is one viable option for taking care of the unwanted elderly. The greatest disadvantage to this option is that you are likely to be one of those unwanted elderly.

You can pray that those programs are preserved, or you can plan on being euthanized by your kids or your spouse, or you can hope that you get ran over by a rich person who'll have to take care of you for the rest of your life. Or you can continue reading this book and begin making rational plans to deal with this risk.

4: Risking Retirement

Retirement is a risk. Like any risk, it must be managed. I am going to teach you how to manage a financially successful retirement. Although there is more to retirement than finances, money is connected to almost everything that makes for an enjoyable retirement, not least of which is freedom from worry.

When you retire, managing your finances changes from accumulating money to deploying money. When you're accumulating money, the main problem is determining how best to invest it without eating up all of the time that you would like to spend developing your career (and then there's spending time with the spouse, kids, relatives and all that other inane crap). Most people do some minimal research to find an appropriate mutual fund and let it go on auto pilot as they deposit as much as possible into a tax-free account. Thankfully, due to unique historical circumstances, that plan has worked well for millions of people

Managing your money in retirement is completely different from accumulating money when you're younger. Retirement requires intelligent, conservative investing and, above all, avoiding unnecessary risks. Before retirement, you depended on your work, so you put a great deal of effort into planning and developing your career—college, professional training, apprenticeships, long hours of uncompensated learning. But in retirement, you depend on your money working for you instead of you working for your money, so you should put as much effort into planning for that as you once put into your career. Unfortunately, people aren't good at planning for the next thirty years, especially if it involves preparing for your possible infirmity and eventual death. For much of our lives, work and other obligations have done the planning for us. People who have gone into work every morning and somehow dealt with the problems as they arise hope that their retirement problems can be dealt with in the same way. Instead of planning how to keep from running out of money, most people think they'll cross that bridge when they come to it. Most people will put more effort into planning for a vacation than they will for their retirement. That is not a recipe for success. If that's your approach, good luck, God bless, and please don't call when the money runs out. I'll only say that I tried to warn you.

In retirement, you must make sure that you have a reliable income stream to cover your necessary expenses. Some inexperienced twits will tell you that you should have an "income-replacement rate." For example, a common figure is 80% of your pre-retirement income. This is nonsense. The amount that we want in retirement may have little to do with our pre-retirement incomes. Some titans of business will retire to the ascetic life of a monk. While those who made small, but dependable incomes may have saved enough for retirement to live like kings. You have to look at your life in retirement and determine what income that requires.

Of course, you want it to cover the necessities, but it should also allow you to do most of the things you dreamed of when you were working. This means that you need a realistic idea about what your expenses will be in comparison to the income stream that you can expect your assets to produce. This stream of income needs to last your entire life and it must be able to withstand predictable downturns and crises and have some extra for the unexpected. Most people have a hard time planning ahead a few months, and while you are working with a steady income, that short-term focus has served you fairly well. Now to be successful, you must think ahead to how your life will change throughout your retirement and make sure that you have the stream of income you want through every stage of your retirement.

There are four kinds of risks to your retirement.
1. You simply didn't save enough money for your entire life.
2. "Sequence of returns." This means that losses occurring in the early part of your retirement are much worse than losses later in your retirement.
3. Inflation could eat away at the value of every dollar you have saved until the cost of living is twice as much as you expected.
4. An unavoidable economic catastrophe.

The first, second and third risk is dealt with by the conservative investing strategy outlined in this book. We will also do what we can to protect you from the fourth, but such catastrophes are often unpredictable, and could be almost anything from early global warming to the zombie apocalypse. Or maybe, just all at once, everybody decides they don't give a fuck at the same time.

Preliminary Steps

I'm going to try to curtail my smart-ass remarks so that we can move quickly through setting up a financial model for your retirement. But before we get into the details of a financially successful retirement, let's take the first concrete step in changing from accumulation to retirement. If you still have money in an old work 401(k), move it into an IRA. This is especially important if you've had multiple jobs and have left multiple 401(k)s. The simplest way to do this is with a trustee-to-trustee transfer into a rollover IRA. If you call up any of the mutual fund companies or brokerages, such as Vanguard, Fidelity, Ameritrade, T. Rowe Price, TIAA-CREF, or one you already deal with, they will walk you through it.

There are three reasons to do this. First, you are undoubtedly paying some hidden management fees. They are not required to report these fees to you and few of them do, but believe me, the brokerage firms and your human resource department are not doing the administration and record-keeping for free. Second, you will open up a whole new world of investment opportunities. Most 401(k)s restrict your choices to a few big mutual funds. An IRA can invest in any mutual fund, as well as exchange-traded funds (ETFs) and any publicly traded company. For most people, ETFs are a much better choice than the mutual funds provided by your 401(k). Third, it is simpler to have one IRA rather than multiple 401(k)s. When you reach 70 ½ you will be required to take a minimum distribution based on your entire retirement savings. If you have multiple IRA's, you have to make sure that they are all providing the required minimum distribution. If you get it wrong, you pay a large penalty.

Now let's learn how to manage your retirement investments and withdrawals. Let's begin by using a spreadsheet to see what your normal retirement might look like. After that we can look at the predictable risks and try to build in a reasonable margin of safety.

If you don't know a spreadsheet program, your first assignment is to learn one. Quit your whining and just do it. I promise you, a couple hours learning will pay off with years of financial security. Here is one free tutorial on using a spreadsheet: https://multimedia.journalism.berkeley.edu/tutorials/spreadsheets/. There are many more if you search online. Or some people prefer an introductory book. There are many good ones available and almost any will suit your needs. Just go and get one from your local library.

You can use Excel if you already have it on your home computer, but even better is the free spreadsheet program, Sheets, available on Google. Using that, we will model your version of a retirement, then we can introduce various possibilities to see how they might affect you and how you can prepare for them.

Many of the numbers entered into your spreadsheet will need to be calculated by you, but I will give you step-by-step directions. Other numbers, I have calculated using a proprietary system of regression analysis and nonlinear, nonparametric, mixed-effect models.

Your Retirement Timeline

Go to https://www.ssa.gov/oact/population/longevity.html to get a rough estimate of your life expectancy. For another site that shows you the predicted longevity of you and your spouse, go to http://www.longevityillustrator.org/. Consider your general health and that of your close relatives. Consider the healthfulness of your lifestyle. Make a best guess for the longest you're likely to live. Keep in mind, that on average, one out of ten live past age 95. If you're a couple, you have a 20% chance that one of you will live past 95.

Create a spreadsheet with a column for each year from retirement until the longest you think you'll live. Create a row each for the following: **Necessary Spending**, **Discretionary Spending**, **Health Spending**.

	2020	2021	2022	2023	2024	2025	2026	2027...
Necessary								
Discretionary								
Health								

You can go here to see examples of this table. If you wish, you can copy one of these into your Google Sheets and adjust it for your own situation.

Determine Your Necessary Spending During Retirement.

Many people simply estimate their retirement spending by taking 80% of their preretirement income. As a quick rule of thumb, this is a good approximation for the average, however it is wildly inaccurate for any specific case. For example, wealthy people can easily get by on 60-70% of the income, while poor people will struggle with 100%. Getting an accurate estimate of your spending is too important to leave to a quick rule of thumb.

Also estimating your spending by just looking at your preretirement income is next to useless for managing the risks of retirement. To manage risks, you need to separate out your necessary spending from your discretionary spending. In a time of crises--either personal crises from health expenses or social crises such as another great recession or reducing Social Security—you may want to cut back to just your necessary spending for a couple of years. We'll discuss this in more detail in later in this chapter and in chapter 12 A Downturn.

Determining your necessary spending is a very touchy subject. One person may see expensive wines, eating out and a lake home as necessary. Another person with a green thumb and a hunting license may see groceries as discretionary. Forget any puritanical moral judgments when calculating this. You want to determine what you regard as necessary in order to have a pleasant retirement, not what an ascetic saint regards as necessary.

You'll want at least three months of data to get an accurate read on your current expenditures. This requires some work on your part, but it is essential. You are establishing your financial security for the rest of your life. If it's done correctly, it will get you through some of your most vulnerable periods. Isn't it worth a little time to get it right? Think of it this way: remember all the planning and preparation that you put into your career from your mid-twenties until you retired 40 years later. Shouldn't you be ready to put as much work into preparing for the next 30 years?

Identify and add up all the expenditures that are necessary for a comfortable life. Many people can get this off their credit card or checking account. If you tend to use cash, start immediately to keep track of what you spend and do it for three months. You can do this while you continue to read this book. Reading ahead will help you to understand why it's important to collect this information.

You'll want to include housing, a mortgage if that is still applicable, property taxes, insurance, utilities, and predictable repairs and maintenance. Transportation, such as car payments, gas, insurance and maintenance and repairs. Food, without the luxury items and only as much eating out as you consider necessary for a pleasant life. TIAA has a nice budget worksheet that separates essential and discretionary spending at https://www.tiaa.org/public/pdf/advice-planning/tools-calculators/A125820_budgeting_worksheet.pdf. Add up your health care costs separately, since we will enter that on its own spreadsheet row.

Put in the annual amount for your necessary spending in the first cell and use a formula to increase the amount in each subsequent cell in the row by an estimate of inflation, let's say 2.5%. You should now have a row giving you your necessary spending for each year of your life.

	2020	2021	2022	2023	2024	2025	2026	2027...
Necessary	70000	71750	73544	75382	77267	79199	81179	83208
Discretionary								
Health								

Discretionary Spending

For the discretionary spending, think about your retirement in terms of stages. For most people, retirement spending can be divided into three stages. Early retirement, lasting around ten years, usually sees the most spending on all those activities that you dreamed of while working: travel, golf, hobbies. The second stage usually goes from 75 to 85. This is when expenses are the least. The third stage lasts for the rest of your life and has the highest spending for health care.

Take your time thinking about the amount of your discretionary spending in early retirement. Thinking about that, planning all the fun things you will do and budgeting for them are almost as much fun as actually doing them. Determine the approximate cost of your fun things for each of the first ten years of your retirement. Include estimates for the cost of moving, if that's part of your plan, as well as new golf clubs, skis, National Park passes, and so on. You might want to create an extra row to put notes on what you planned to spend. That way you can easily update your spreadsheet if you move a year later than planned or go to Italy a year earlier.

For the second stage of your retirement, consider a reasonable yearly amount of discretionary spending based on how you live at your most comfortable. For most retirees, comfort is the watchword for this second stage. Also put in a little extra for new and unpredictable items. Ten years ago, who could have known that you would need a smart phone and high-speed internet?

For the third stage, discretionary spending is usually at a minimum. Comfort usually means staying home rather than eating out. You don't want to learn any new-fangled gadgets, no matter how necessary people may think they are. The most expensive spending will be in health care, which we will cover next.

You will have determined this spending in today's dollars, so you will need to account for inflation. Multiply the numbers for discretionary spending by the estimate of inflation, e.g. 2.5% for each year out from today.

Healthcare

In your health care row, you can put the amount of health care spending that you found doing your budget. If you are not yet on Medicare, you'll want to look at the different options, fees and copays for Part B and D. A typical annual cost would be $5,200. You should put this number in your 65-year-old health care cell and then use a formula to increase the cost by 3.5% each year through the first and second stage. In the third stage, your health care costs are likely to go up, sometimes precipitously. Studies show that a good estimate will average out to $20,000 a year in today's dollars. To get an estimate of what that would be with inflation, you can use the FV formula in Excel. Under the year that you turn 85, put a version of the following formula: =FV(3.5%,20,0,-20000). 3.5 is the assumed inflation rate for medical, 20 is the number of years in the future, 20000 is the cost in the year you are 65. Adjust that formula to fit your situation and put that into the cell under your 85th year. Fill in the rest of the healthcare cells until the end of your life, with a formula multiplying the previous year by 3.5% to account for inflation in health care which has been more than general inflation.

	2020	2021	2022	2023	2024	2025	2026	2027…
Necessary	70000	71750	73544	75382	77267	79199	81179	83208
Discretionary	30000	50000	31519	42000	33114	33942	60000	35661
		Italy		Mexico			London	
Health	5200	5382	5570	5765	5967	6176	6392	6616

Income

Now add rows for each of your guaranteed income sources, such as a pension, Social Security, annuity, etc. If you're married, be sure to include your spouse's income sources. Fill in the appropriate amounts for the rest of your expected life.

Add rows for **Investment Income** and for **Investment Money**. In the first cell of **Investment Money**, put how much money you have in IRAs, and non-IRA investments. In the first cell of **Investment Income** put a formula for *Investment Money* * .06.

For the second cell of **Investment Money** put the formula for the following: *Investment Money from the previous Investment Money cell + Guaranteed Incomes + Investment Income – Necessary Spending – Discretionary Spending – Health Care*.

Copy the second cell of Investment Money and paste into all the cells representing the rest of your life.

Copy the first cell of Investment Income and paste into the rest of the cells.

It's also nice to have a chart showing the trends in your wealth. Use the numbers in Investment Money to create a line chart.

	2020	2021	2022	2023	2024	2025	2026	2027…
Spending								
Necessary	70000	71750	73544	75382	77267	79199	81179	83208
Discretionary	30000	50000	31519	42000	33114	33942	60000	35661
		Italy		Mexico			London	
Health	5200	5382	5570	5765	5967	6176	6392	6616
Income								
Pension	18000	18000	18000	18000	18000	18000	18000	18000
Soc Sec	24000	24480	24970	25469	25978	26498	27028	27568
Invest Income	60000	59808	58317	56573	55186	53559	51673	48620
Invest Money	1000000	996800	971956	942879	919773	892654	861210	810340
Withdraw	32000	24844	29077	23106	27119	31444	50870	57135

Withdrawing Your Money

Add a row for the amount you need to **Withdraw** every year. In this put the sum of **Necessary Spending**, **Discretionary Spending** and **Health Spending** and subtract your **Guaranteed Incomes** and **Investment Income**. That is how much you will need to withdraw from your investment money every year. If your investments are up, you should withdraw a lump sum for the year and put it into a cash equivalent, such as a money market fund, short-term treasury ETF, a saving account, or a conservative bond fund like Fidelity's FCONX. If your investments are down, pull out 1/12 of the annual withdrawal amount every month.

The worst thing in retirement is being forced to withdraw money when the market is down. In order to protect yourself from that, you should have one year of what you would need to withdraw for your necessary and discretionary spending plus a second year of what you would need to withdraw for just necessary spending in a safe cash-equivalent account. You should withdraw from this only when the market is down as described in Chapter 12 Downturn.

There are several myths and unproven theories about how to withdraw your money. First, there is no such thing as a perfectly risk-free withdrawal rate. There is always some risk. A 4% withdrawal rate has become a rule of thumb, but such a rule of thumb is unnecessary when you have taken the time to create a model as we have above. In most cases, people can safely withdraw more than 4%. If you are ready to be flexible in your spending, you can probably withdraw 6% just as safely as the inflexible person could withdraw 4%. The main point is that if you're not running out of money in the spreadsheet model, then it makes no difference whether you are withdrawing more or less than 4%.

It is a mistake to only withdraw interest and dividend money. Many people like this because they never have to touch their capital. But you would need to have quite a bit more money to invest if you want to live off the interest and dividend alone. And investments that produce enough interest and dividends to live on are usually not your safest investments. We are trying to design an investment portfolio that produces the money you need for as long as you need it with the minimum of risk. The best investment portfolio will provide the income for your withdrawals from a mix of selling stocks, dividends and interest.

There are funds that will manage the withdrawal for you. For example, JP Morgan has a SmartSpending fund that will withdraw a combination of interest, dividend and capital so that you will reach zero by the fund's maturity date in 2050. At the start of each year, they will set a withdrawal rate that the retiree can count on. If you don't have the time or inclination to follow the program in this book, that's an acceptable alternative.

A popular theory is to use "buckets" in your withdrawal strategy. This has been disproven. A thorough test of various bucket schemes confirmed that the best strategy is to have a fund of ready cash and to invest the rest in diversified assets that are periodically rebalanced. That is the strategy that will be described in subsequent chapters.

Reviewing and Updating Your Model

Add one row to your spreadsheet model and label this **6 Month**. In those cells put a formula to take the average of this year's and next year's **Investment Money**. Every 6 months, you should add up all your Investments and compare it to the **Investment Money** in your model. If there is a large shortfall, you should determine what went wrong. If the market went down and you are following the investment strategy described in this book, then that is just the vagaries of the market. If you are spending more than expected, look to see if you need to update your future spending or if this is just a one-time thing. On the other hand, if you are more than 30% ahead of you predicted Investment Money, then you should look for more ways to enjoy your money.

Once a year, you should replace the calculated model for your Investment Income with your actual amount. See how that affects your chart.

The idea that you can just make a plan at the start and follow it for the rest of your retirement is wrong. You should check this model every six months and update it every year. And you should consider how this changes your retirement plan. Think of it like a boat trip. You may have looked at the map and planned your trip, but if you see that you are ahead or behind schedule, hitting heavy weather, running out of provisions or carrying unnecessary ballast, you adjust your plans accordingly.

Using Your Model to Test Scenarios

Now you have a nice model. If everything goes as predicted, this is what your retirement money will do. However, one thing you can be sure of is that things will never go as predicted, so this is a model that lets you test various events that could happen.

Under these predictable conditions, your wealth should never get to zero. If it does or even gets close, you must find alternative means of income such as a job or a longevity annuity and you should reduce your discretionary spending.

We'll use this model to see what happens in a worst-case scenario. We'll start by looking at what happens if the market goes down at the worst possible time. In your first Investment Income cell, replace .06 with -.20. The stock market has gone down more in the past, but I'm going to show you how to ensure that this is the worst downturn that you will suffer. The year after a downturn is almost always up, but let's put another smaller downturn into your third Investment Income cell by replacing .06 with -.10. Next in 2026, change your Health Care cell from 1.035 to 1.40 because you just got hit with a big Medicare increase. And starting in 2034, decrease your Social Security by 40%.

Save this new sheet under a different name and keep your original sheet unchanged.

If you still don't outlive your money, then your main problem is learning how to invest so that you have at least 6% return for most years and how to protect yourself from a downturn of more than 20%. All of which will be covered in the rest of this book.

If you run out of money in this worst-case scenario, you'll have to look at additional ways to make income AND find ways to cut back on your discretionary spending. The worst way to deal with this potential catastrophe is to continue on and hope for the best. The second worst way to deal with this is to try to increase the return you make on your investments. If you increase your investment returns, you will increase your investment risk, that's just how the market works. If you increase your risks, you increase not only the likelihood of losing capital, but also the likelihood that you will panic and do something stupid such as exiting the market at the bottom of a downturn and staying out during the fastest part of the recovery. Trying to increase your investment returns just because you need the money is a bonehead move. The market doesn't care about your needs. It cares about the amount of risk you are willing to take. And a retired investor who is already unprepared for an economic downturn is not a good candidate for increased risk.

Income Generation: The Encore Career

Let's try another test scenario with your spreadsheet model. Take your worst-case scenario worksheet. Add another row right below your guaranteed income. Put $10,000 in each cell until you're 80. Add that cell to the cells showing your **Investment Money** and subtract it from the cells showing your **Withdrawal**. Look at your chart.

Notice how a steady income of as little as $10,000 smooths out your downturns and lessens the lowest your wealth will go. Unless you have enough money saved to weather any economic and personal crisis, everyone should consider working enough to make $10,000 a year or at least being prepared to.

That might not be your idea of retirement. You might think that your retirement will be resting in your easy chair after your many years of labor, sipping a beer, wandering out to your hammock and taking a nap before going to eat the Early Bird special, after which you'll fall asleep with the nightly news blaring. This view of retirement is as outmoded as your grandfather's vacuum-tube record-player.

Improvements in health and increased employment choices have changed the retirement landscape. Today, almost forty percent of those 65-70 will work and about a quarter of those between 70 and 75. Some continue to work because they have to, but most simply enjoy working and the activity and interaction that it involves. Surveys of those over 65 who are still working show that seventy percent report the highest level of job satisfaction. Working after retirement age relieves the boredom and purposelessness that often accompanies retirement. And it has the added benefit of making your retirement more secure.

There are many books discussing an encore career, but you can probably come up with your own realistic possibilities. Some retirees just continue to work part-time at their old jobs. For example, I've always kept my hand in the drug dealing business. Twice a year, I use old contacts to smuggle some cocaine into the U.S. and that's enough for me to make over $10,000 a year.

Many decide to start their own business. Those over 65 are the most likely to be self-employed. One especially popular option is rental property or even an Airbnb casita. When you run your own business, you can put as much time into it as you choose. And if your business takes off, you can always hire people to take the bulk of the work and still leave you time to enjoy your retirement.

One of the neighbors in my little retirement village has bought a list of elderly people's phone numbers. With just two or three phone calls, four at most, from an unlisted number, he is able to get someone to send him $2000, supposedly to get their grandson out of jail. Five suckers like that, and you've got your $10,000 for the year. My neighbor sees it as a kind of stupidity tax and a couple thousand seems like a small amount to pay for the important lesson that you're too demented to look after your own money.

Many retired people are able to turn their hobbies into a money-making venture. They make a profit from something they love to do. A friend of mine had always loved collecting antiques and she now has a nice little income to supplement her retirement by making fake antiques. If you already know how to *spot* a fake antique, it's easy to learn how to *make* a fake.

Another friend always loved hunting and so he's become a contract killer. It usually consumes a week of his time, what with travel, research, surveillance and planning, but he only needs to do it once a year. There are those who have some moral qualms about this, but every job has some minor drawbacks. I'm a lousy shot, or I'd do this myself.

Perhaps the most satisfying is to make some money through your own creativity. Not everyone is a Picasso, but most have some creativity that others are willing to pay good money for. It could be playing music at a local restaurant during high tourist season, or like me, you could write a book. There are many niche markets that can be reached through Kindle Unlimited and which will give you $10,000 a year for part time work. They are always looking for some soft-core erotica, military science fiction or interracial romance.

Cutting Back on Discretionary Spending

This is not your grandfather's or even your father's retirement. The days of a predictable, stable retirement appear to be over. Most don't have pensions. Social Security and Medicare can't be counted on. Politics seems unable to solve any crisis. The economy is more powerful, but more unpredictable than ever. Everything that is solid melts into air. You must be prepared for the new, volatile unpredictable, risk-filled retirement.

For the 30 or so years that you'll be retired, it would be unwise to expect no economic catastrophe. In the last thirty years there have been four meltdowns that have devastated the financially vulnerable. Personally, I believe that the chance of economic catastrophe has increased while our ability to deal with it has almost vanished. Interest rates have been so low and deficits so high, it's hard to see how any interest-rate finagling and deficit-spending shenanigans could help us out of another economic disaster. Of course, the worst may never come. There is no predicting the future. But we would be wise to plan for any catastrophe as likely as this is.

An encore career should be your first line of defense in an economic disaster—your Plan A--but it's not practical for everyone. Some people have a disability. Others just hate to work. A few are blackballed by limp-dicked, two-faced fatcats all because of a little murder rap. If Plan A is impractical or the catastrophe is severe, controlling your discretionary spending is Plan B.

The worst move you can make during an economic disaster is to withdraw funds to live on. That is called selling low, and most investors frown on it. The best move you can make during an economic disaster is to start investing as soon as it's over. Those periods usually see the greatest rate of increase. If you cut down on discretionary spending, you do less of the worst move and more of the best move. Instead of spending money on a vacation, sailboat, new wife, etc., you save your money to invest as the market recovers.

Many retirees have had to cut back on spending at some time in their retirement. People rarely feel that they are unhappier because of it. Indeed, many retirees find that they just naturally spend less money than they anticipated without any sense of deprivation.

You should also remember that you will not be the only one who is undergoing this economic disaster. It is likely that any catastrophe would affect everyone except the upper 1/10 of percent (although they are the ones who typically cause the economic shitstorm, the usually come out smelling like roses). Your friends will also be skipping vacations, cutting back on expenses, looking for ways to save money and learning to think like our grandparents did during the depression. There will be a certain camaraderie amongst the afflicted.

Living frugally can be fun, especially if it only lasts a few years. Thinking of the ways that we could live more frugally--caretaking a farmhouse, growing our own food, cutting off your freeloading daughter, rotating dinner parties instead of restaurants—can be exhilarating. Do some planning now. Investigate some possibilities. You should be able to drastically cut back on your spending as soon as necessary. While others are still recovering from the shock of an economic crisis and trying to delude themselves that it will soon be over, you will be ready to put plan B into action.

Those who will do best will have planned out and are ready to implement both plan A and plan B. You must know how you will generate income and how you will cut back on spending.

5: D-I-Y

My years at Madoff

I started on Wall Street at Madoff Securities. Yes, that Madoff. My wife had gone to school with one of Bernie's traders and I was hired even though I had no experience. My first job was recording and filing legitimate trades, but after I demonstrated my ability to be creative with record keeping, I was transferred to the private fund and worked under Bill DiPascali on what would be revealed as the biggest Ponzi scheme in history.

When you think of someone being robbed, you usually picture the fear, confusion and anger of the victim. Ponzi schemes don't work like that. Instead of fear and anger, the victims exhibit gratitude and appreciation. Bernie's victims were glad to have been let in on this exclusive fund where investors consistently made above market returns. A day rarely went by without some victim calling to check on their investment and telling me that God would bless me for the work I was doing. After all, the money that was robbed didn't go to me or Bernie--we just made a normal Wall Street wage--it went to another victim. In a typical transferal, money would come in from some wealthy, high-living multi-millionaire and part of it would go out to a retired widow who was able to spend her days working for a charity instead of worrying about money. Both victims, the multi-millionaire and the retired widow were grateful.

Bernie was the face of the scheme, but the actual work was done by people like me. We weren't master criminals. We were far from masters of the universe, wizards of lies, or wolves of wall street, we were just the usual collection of office workers found in any Wall Street firm. The only difference was that instead of actually trading, we just created the paperwork that made it look like we were trading.

Of course, everybody in the office knew that we were doing something illegal, but you would be amazed by people's capacity to delude themselves. Practically every worker there had some of their own money "invested." They were a friendly, hard-working bunch, but occasionally you would see a haunted look in someone's eyes that would linger for many days. And then there were the suicides. We were a small office, but we averaged two suicides a year, and one year in the early 90s, we had four.

Nothing good can last forever and this was no exception. In Dec. 2008, Bernie started handing out bonuses early and soon it all fell apart. The FBI arrested him and they made the life-savings of thousands of people disappear in a blink. One minute you are rich with more money than you could ever spend, and the next moment you are destitute. One minute you are an astute investor and the next, ignorant sucker. One minute, first-class travel, college funds, financial security; the next, anxiously awaiting bankrupt proceedings.

The worst was that Bernie was made the scapegoat for all of Wall Street's excesses. As though Bernie created it instead of merely being its product. Like Vice in the Medieval morality plays, the audience delights in an evil personified. And Bernie personified Wall Street. But Bernie didn't corrupt Wall Street, Wall Street corrupted Bernie.

Everybody knew that Bernie was breaking the law. They just happened to be wrong about the law that was being broken. Everybody knew that you couldn't make such consistent returns without some insider trading. And everybody was ready to profit from that. But it turned out that Bernie was completely innocent of insider trading. It was just an old-fashioned Ponzi scheme. Insider trading only hurts the "dumb money," the ordinary trader. So, everybody is ready to go along with that. A Ponzi scheme hits the "smart money," the millionaires, banks and hedge funds that were Bernie's victims. I leave it to you to decide which is immoral.

Strangely enough, the Madoff scandal did not hurt my career. No, quite the opposite. Within a year, I had set up a little private hedge fund that catered to the ultra-wealthy. They liked people who were creative with their record keeping and could keep their mouth shut. It grew into the SmashWealth that everyone knows today. However, not everyone came out as good.

I felt sorry for Frank DiPascali. Facing a long prison sentence, he naturally, turned state's witness against his former friends and colleagues. That is one difference between the Mafia and Wall Street. There is no *omerta*. The judge in the case was very skeptical of Frank's stories and he faced long years in prison, so he reached out to me for help.

You might say that Frank was the first person I murdered. Of course, he was a willing participant, but then I think that all murder victims willingly participate in some way. From my perspective, my wife willingly participated in her own murder by planning my murder, but I suppose we all have our own view of morality.

Frank was awaiting sentencing and if he died before that, his case would be nullified. Then his ill-gotten fortune would pass on to his family instead of being seized by the government. Also, he'd had a slow-growing cancer for many years, so it wasn't hard to arrange for it to look like natural causes.

I learned a lot that came in handy later. "Cleaning" the scene. Staging the scene. When to call the coroner and which coroner to call. All the modern bureaucracy of dying and how to manipulate it.

Financial Advisors

There was nothing unusual in the case of Bernie Madoff. The only reason he was caught was because of a global meltdown. As Warren Buffet says, only when the tide goes out do you discover who's been swimming naked. Ponzi schemes are unusual, but financial advisors are notorious for fleecing the individual investor. I could recount the kickbacks, swindles, scandals, bankruptcies, insider trading, payola, bribery, corruption until I was blue in the face. But you only have to look at the recent attempt to require advisors to put clients' needs ahead of their own. Called the fiduciary rule, it would have made financial advisors tell their clients when they are getting a kickback on the investment they are touting. The lobbyists of the financial industry saw to it that it was never put into action.

Why do intelligent investors go to financial advisors? As one expert put it, "Because they're idiots." The whole financial advising industry exists because Americans know next to nothing about investing. Even though our retirement and health care depend on us being able to intelligently invest. The decision not to teach our children in school how to invest, results in a population that is dependent on professional financial advisors. No matter how bad the advisor is, they won't invest all your money in a long-shot, "sure-bet" on a company that nobody's ever heard of; they won't put everything into Krugerrands; they won't keep the money in a box under their mattress waiting for another Great Depression.

Americans are set up to be dependent on financial advisors. They keep us ignorant for that very reason. If you try to kick this dependence, they will explain—with small words and a kindergarten teacher's demeanor—that it's much too complicated. If you try to break free, you're told you need an Ivy-league MBA to understand this shit. Really? Is it more complicated than physics? But they teach us that. How about instead of teaching us geometry, which nobody ever uses, they teach us investing? Or instead of diagraming sentences?

If you already have a financial advisor, then I have one question that will tell you how good he is.

How is he paid?

If you know exactly how your financial advisor is paid, you have a good one. If you don't know, you have a bad one. Simple as that.

Most financial advisors make some of their money off of loads. Loads are kickback to the broker for getting you to buy the investment. Some investments pay higher loads than others. Studies have shown that financial advisors tout investments with loads even when a no-load investment has performed better. You don't want your financial interests standing between a financial advisor and his profit. Your financial interests will get run over.

To make things worse, a financial advisor makes money whenever he buys or sells an investment for you. Even when the market is down, the advisor can generate fees by making trades. And the client is apt to applaud this useless and costly churning, because they think that their advisor is doing something. When in fact, the stinking turd is just generating fees.

I know there are good advisors out there. I met one once. He was a Quaker, did volunteer work and saw to it that every investment he made was to his client's benefit, even if it was at the expense of his own interests. I do believe that these unicorns exist, but I don't think there are very many of them.

You can divide financial advisors into two types. There are those who know nothing about economics or the market. They only learned enough to pass a regulatory exam and that was it. The other type of financial advisor has been thoroughly trained in economics and the workings of the market. You obviously don't want the first type, but most people don't realize that you also don't want the second. These financial advisors embrace the idea taught in Economics 101 and repeated in every subsequent class that they should maximize their profit. Maximum profit is the first law of economics. And the second law is to pay attention to the first law. Unfortunately, the advisor's maximum profit comes at the expense of the investor. The interest of the individual investor and that of the advisor are inherently in conflict. Investors want low, transparent fees; while advisors want high, hidden fees. Investors want few transactions to avoid taxes on profits; advisors want short-term churning. Investors have long-term goals;

advisors are looking for their next paycheck. Advisors are looking to expand the assets they manage, but investors do better when there is less to manage. In general, the better the investment is for the financial advisor, the worse it is for the investor.

You must take control of your own portfolio, BUT it is a good idea to have a financial advisor look over your investments once a year. But you should use a fee-only advisor and do the trading yourself. You can find one through the National Association of Personal Financial Advisors (NAPFA). Members of this organization have pledged to put your interest first. They do not accept any commission for referring a client or selling any particular investment. Their only compensation is the fee you pay them. There is no hidden commission. That is the only way that your interests and the advisor's interests will be aligned.

Get a list of recommended advisors. Check them out on BrokerCheck.finra.org for any disciplinary problems on their record. Then call them up and ask how much it would cost for 1 or 2 hours of their time. It should be around $250 an hour. That initial meeting should be enough to tell if a couple thousand more to pay for a personalized investment plan would be worth it.

By taking control of your own portfolio, you can focus on increasing and preserving your wealth instead of generating fees and attracting new investors. Your understanding of your own risks is better than anyone else's could be. You know when you want to take taxable profits. You are focused on your entire life's timeline. No one is going to care as much about your investments as you.

Obviously, you have to educate yourself. Plenty of people who take control of their own portfolio make bonehead mistakes because they haven't taken the time to educate themselves. That is really the point of this book. To put you in charge.

Don't Buy & Hold Index Funds

For many people, taking control of their portfolio has meant putting all their money into an index fund that mirrors the S&P 500. I laugh with scorn, but really that isn't the worst thing you could do. It's certainly not as bad as letting a financial advisor control your portfolio. However, I'm going to teach you how to do better.

The idea of investing in an index fund came out of a new theory of finance developed at the University of Chicago in the 1960s. It is usually called the efficient market hypothesis. This theory asserts that stock market prices are always accurate reflections of the underlying value of a company. To academics--who study the theory of economics while assiduously avoiding actually engaging in it—the market is always right. This market system which is not a force of nature, not a creation of God, but a man-made, poorly understood system of trading is always right. This system that we know is full of uncertainty and unpredictability is always right. The one that has had a series of bubbles, recessions, crashes and depressions is always right. Really?

These academics claim that the price of a stock is always fairly valued. If a stock is selling too low, buyers will rush in to buy it and raise the price. If the stock is selling too high, traders will sell it and the price will go lower. As soon as a new piece of information that affects the value is discovered, it will be immediately reflected in the price of the stock. With everyone doing similar analysis on the same information, the stock is guaranteed to be fairly valued.

Stock prices move all day in the absence of any new information. Have you ever asked yourself, "What are those Bozos trading on?" According to the efficient market hypothesis, this is simply random motion. This is what gave the title to the immensely popular book promoting this hypothesis, *A Random Walk Down Wall Street* by Professor Burton Malkiel.

Since all prices are fairly valued and any discrepancy is random, investing skill is nothing but luck. Therefore, nobody can consistently beat the market. In that case, the best plan is to buy the entire market instead of trying to pick winners. This is the idea behind an index fund. You cannot consistently predict which stock or even sector you should overweight or underweight. Just accept that when the market goes up, your investment will go up the same amount and when the market goes down so will you.

As part of their long-standing tradition of having their heads up their asses, these academics take the reasonable idea that the market is frequently right to the absurd conclusion that it is always right. The professors love the efficient market hypothesis because it will give them precise, numerical measurements of the state of the economy. They don't care if it's frequently wrong, all that matters is that it's precise. Plus, it has the added advantage that any mispricing can be blamed on government interference, and who today is going to defend the government?

What a wonderful world we would live in if they were right! You wouldn't have to worry about your investments. Your investments would sprout up like dandelions in your lawn and spread to cover your entire estate with a gold-like yellow hue. They would require no thought, no care, no fertilizer, not even water. And upon your retirement, you could pick what you needed and live happily ever after.

But we know from actual experience that it is not true. Did the companies that made up the DOW actually lose half their real value between Oct. 2007 and March 2008? Did your home lose 2/3 of its real value? Did AIG's and Bear Stearn's real value become zero? Of course not!

Obviously, the psychology of the market matters. The market is not some giant calculating system churning out its precise algorithms of value. It is a collection of often irrational investors. When those investors are afraid, the market plummets, no matter what the underlying actual value is. When they are exuberant, the market goes up. Over the long run, the professors may be right. The real value will win out. Unfortunately, if you are retired, you don't have the long run to wait for the real value to win out. Unlike the professors, you have to deal with the market as it is.

Many people have developed a buy-and-hold strategy as they have saved for retirement. This usually has worked well because the investor is working on his career and doesn't have time to pay attention to their investments and also because the investor has a long timeframe so that he have plenty of time to make up for any down years. These are no longer true for the retired investor, so a buy-and-hold is not the optimum strategy.

If the market went up year after year, buy-and-hold would be the perfect strategy and you would not need to educate yourself about investments. You'd just buy your index fund and watch the money roll in. However, the market has never worked like that and it's even less likely to work that way in the near future. In the market crash of 1973-1974, the stock market fell by 60%. It didn't come back until the spring of 1980. A buy-and-hold strategy would have lost the investor money for almost eight years.

A string of high paying years, like we've had recently, makes it more likely that we will have some below normal returns. In the type of market volatility that we seem to be heading for, the investor must be strategic. To lower risks, you must sometimes pull back on your investments and put more into cash, so that you have money to buy the bargains when the market goes down. There have been many times when the most money is made by having ready cash in a downturn rather than being fully invested and holding on.

Just like in poker, it's sometimes best to stay pat and play the hand you're dealt. But nobody would suggest that you always do that. Sometimes the smartest move is to get rid of your bad cards and have the dealer give you some new ones.

There was a time when the buy-and-hold strategy made more sense. It wasn't that long ago when it cost you hundreds of dollars to sell one stock and buy another. That has all changed. Today you can get on the internet and buy stocks without incurring any fee at all. This is a momentous change. Removing fees from an economic system is like removing friction from a physical system. Everything moves more freely. With freely traded ETFs you are free to move in and out of entire sectors as you see fit. That doesn't mean that you should buy and sell willy-nilly. You have to be disciplined and to follow a thoughtful strategy. But it does mean that there is no reason to hang on to a bad investment when you know that better investments are out there.

In stocks, buy-and-hold can become personal. Selling a stock is seen as admitting defeat. There is always the hope that someday it will pay off if only you hold it long enough. And this is often true, it does pay off eventually, but you also have to look at all the other investments that would have made more money. While you were hanging on to your stock until you finally made a nickel, the S&P has doubled in value.

Even worse than index funds are actively managed funds. Study after study has shown that actively managed funds do no better than index funds and usually worse. Every year, there are a few who do better than the market, but with thousands of actively managed funds, some are going to beat the market just by random chance. It is more likely that this year's best performing fund will be next year's worst than that it will repeat its success. There is no evidence that an actively managed fund can consistently beat the market. In fact, when you subtract the fees that they charge, they do worse. And they are always worse for your taxes since their constant buying and selling generate taxable capital gains even when the fund as a whole is losing you money.

You can take control of your own investments. You can take control of your own money. I'm not going to say it's easy. It's hard because nobody has really taught you anything about it. Everything important, you've had to figure out for yourself. It's like the first time in the back seat with Marge. You feel like you should know what you're doing, but you really don't. And you're embarrassed to admit it, even to yourself.

We are conflicted about money. Money is the root of all evil, but a necessary evil. You should be ashamed for wanting it; ashamed for even thinking about it; and especially, ashamed for not having it. Because you'd better have some of that evil shit. In this country, if you're old and sick or might be old and sick at some point, you'd better have money. If you want to be treated with any respect, you'd better have money. If you'd like to have an old age with dignity, you'd better have money.

You don't have to be three months behind on your payments or living out of your car or have hit bottom in order to decide that you must take control of your own money. You don't have to have an epiphany on the road to Damascus or narrowly escape death. You just have to be sick of hearing your own rationalizations for your own self-imposed limitations. You just have to decide to be in control of your own life.

What kind of guy do you want to be? Do you want to be the guy sitting in front of a shot glass in his bathrobe saying to his dog, "I'm worried about that money thing, but hey what can ya do?" Or do you want to be the guy with options, who's in control instead of a victim of circumstances? Do you want to be somebody who's afraid of money or in control of money?

Once in broad daylight in the middle of Wall Street with traders who knew me going by, my wife grabbed me by the balls and yelled, "Be a man!" I want this book to be like that for you. Take control of your own investments. Take control of your money. Be a man!

6: Psychological Problems

How could I have been so stupid? Every investor has asked themselves that question at some time, usually many times. The simple answer is, "Because you're human," and humans were not made to correctly understand the risk of investing. Evolution has shaped us to avoid risk rather than manage it. The monkey who immediately ran up the tree because he heard stirrings in the bush has survived, while the monkey who considered all the possible sources of that sound and tried to determine the likelihood of it being dangerous was eaten.

Our view of the market and our reactions to losses and profits are profoundly shaped by that monkey that ran up the tree. It is a mistake to think that you react to market moves in completely rational ways. Being confronted by a loss or anticipating a gain is a physiological event. Even if the monkey could give good, rational reasons for running up that tree, he still felt the shudder of fear when he heard the stirrings. You're still a monkey, when it comes to investing.

Emotions

When we risk money, we arouse some of the most powerful physiological reactions we can feel, our emotions. Fear, greed, envy, hope are among the most prominent. But there's also anticipation, anxiety, bitterness, boredom, cockiness, conformism, and the beat goes on. When you win, you are filled with elation and when you lose, regret. There is nothing wrong with these emotions. After all, they are the reasons we are investing in the first place. We want to feel elation and avoid regret. The problems come from discounting them or worse, completely ignoring them. Instead of acknowledging that we are emotional animals and managing those emotions, we pretend that we are rational-decision machines and thereby give those emotions an unrecognized free rein.

Most of the errors that you have made and will make come from your unacknowledged emotions. The real question to ask yourself is not "How could I have been so stupid?" but "How could I have been so emotional?" Most of the moves that make no investing sense, make perfect emotional sense.

We see the world through an emotional filter. Losses are not just a negative number in the profit column, they are affronts to our intelligence that provoke our fears of failing. Profits are not abstract numbers; they are a vindication of our hopes and the last laugh at those who laughed at us. If I win here, what can't I win at? And if I lose here, aren't I destined to lose at everything?

Even when we feel most rational in our decision-making, we are apt to be driven by hidden emotions. We might start to rationally investigate an investment, but not go too deep because of the rush of adrenalin that comes from anticipating our winnings. We might ignore compelling evidence because of the gratification we feel in having our preconceptions confirmed. We might not anticipate what would happen if we were wrong because thinking of our own fallibility made us feel anxious. Behind every cold calculation is a hidden emotional tempest.

We see the world through emotion-tinged glasses. We overreact or underreact as our emotions push us. Our unacknowledged emotional reactions overwhelm the self-control that is necessary for rational investment decisions. And so, we sell when the market is low and buy when the market is high, not because of any rational strategy but simply because we are afraid of losing more when it is low or afraid of missing out when it is high. This is the source of most of our investing mistakes and a significant drain on our investments.

You can see these emotions every day in the market. In the real economic world, things change slowly. Most of the economic information that we get fluctuates between "moderately disappointing" and "fairly good." And yet the market swings wildly with each slight gradation. The market is 100 times more volatile than the underlying economy that it's supposed to represent. The added volatility is our human emotions at work.

You can't control the market, but you can control your reaction to it. Everyone who starts to invest and pays attention to the results will learn something about the market, but only a select few will learn about themselves. Your rational mind can master the skills and knowledge necessary to make good investments, but you will never become a superior investor unless you learn about the human flaws and psychological snares that will subvert the best-laid plans. You can spend years mastering fundamental analysis and chart interpretation, you can learn all the latest statistical techniques and study the careers of the top CEOs, but it will all come to naught when the monkey gets scared and scampers up that tree.

A recent study looking at investor's returns for the last 50 years concluded that the average investor made under 5% per year while the market averaged a return of more than 9%. With compounding, this means that the average investor is losing more than one and a half million dollars on a half-million investment over 20 years. The primary reason for the lost money is because the average investor makes bad decisions due to emotional responses. For example, they wait to sell until they have extensive losses, and they stay out after a downturn when the market is usually rising the fastest.

Know thyself is always a difficult endeavor, but it is especially difficult for the smartest and most accomplished people. Isaac Newton lost a bundle in a speculative bubble. "I can calculate the motions of the heavenly bodies, but not the madness of people," Newton said. But even some of our greatest chroniclers of the human condition, Mark Twain, Charles Dickens, Leo Tolstoy were notoriously bad investors. Understanding others is easier than understanding ourselves. Understanding the heavens or even everyday life doesn't help us to understand the investing mistakes to which we are prone. That is why doctors, lawyers, business executive, scientists and engineers make the worst investors. They understand their field and are unaware of how little they understand themselves.

You first have to learn about yourself before you learn about the market. If you are afraid of uncertainty, avoid admitting mistakes, need to feel in control, are fooled by flimsy evidence that confirms your bias, prone to rationalization, or certain that your hopes will work out, then you will never be a superior investor, although you will almost certainly convince yourself that you are, despite all the evidence to the contrary. An old saying sums it up, "It ain't what we don't know that gets us in trouble. It's what we know for sure that just ain't so." Some people will never learn that lesson and will spend their lives sure that they were born unlucky, or the system is fixed, or the system is broken, or somebody has it out for them. Some people will learn after years of expensive mistakes. The superior investor will learn this right now. You are an emotionally unbalanced monkey and so are all the other investors.

Study after study, by researcher after researcher, in field after field have all concluded that humans are emotionally unbalanced monkeys. Bananas put us in the mood for love. Music makes us buy beyond our means. Our moral assessment of a situation is dependent on the last movie that we saw. Our definition of rationality depends on the time of day. And, we are enthusiastically wrong about our own state of mind. Not that there's anything wrong with that. I have a great admiration for emotionally unbalanced monkeys.

Emotions come in many flavors and varieties. I will group them into two kinds: those based on fear and those based on narcissism.

Fear

The science-fiction classic, Dune, taught us that "Fear is the mind-killer." The Hitchhikers Guide to the Galaxy" had "Don't Panic" emblazoned on its cover. Could the science-fiction writers be onto something?

Falling markets evoke fear. Often we don't know why they are falling. The very idea of a correction means that there is no external reason. The market, for some reason, decides to correct itself. The market didn't seem to need correction yesterday, but today it does. Was it acting rationally before and is now irrationally correcting, or is the correction a rational response to past irrationality? Who will ever know? We don't know the cause; we don't know what made it start; we don't know when it will stop; we don't know how much we will lose, or why. The natural reaction to all of this is fear. It's in our DNA, below our consciousness, out of our rational control.

Fear of Markets and Money

Some fear the market itself, especially those who have lived through a turbulent downturn. Some are even afraid of money. We feel we should know how money works, but too often we don't. We are ashamed to admit our ignorance, ashamed of having money, ashamed of wanting more. It is the root of all evil, we are told, and who wouldn't be afraid of that?

This is a fear you must get over immediately. Money is just a tool for doing all the things you want to do. You can have money and still protect the environment, love your wife and children, pet puppies and smell the roses. Certainly, people can become too concerned about money, and that is something to be afraid of, but that more often comes from insecurities about money than from having too much. The point of this book is to make you more secure about money and then maybe you can be even better at caring for the environment, your family, puppies and roses.

Fear of Uncertainty

More serious and more pervasive is a fear of uncertainty. Since investing always involves risk, it also involves uncertainty. The ability to tolerate uncertainty is essential to the superior investor. The average investor wants to be right on every trade, so he fabricates a certainty where it doesn't really exist. This fabricated certainty is at the heart of most investment mistakes. The superior investor is an *uncertain* investor. The average-asshole investor is always *certain*.

The *uncertain* superior investor knows that he is placing a bet that may or may not pay off. He is ready to get out of the bet if it turns out that he's wrong. The certain investor, the average-asshole, knows that he's right and when the bet doesn't pay off, he keeps betting more in an attempt to finally prove he was right all along.

The uncertain investor knows that the market is not entirely rational, so he is never surprised when irrationality rears its ugly head. The certain investor believes that the market is rational and if it doesn't act as predicted, he just hasn't figured out a complex enough system. He drops one system for investing after huge losses and picks up another even more esoteric system for predicting the "rational" market, until that one also fails and he loses even more in order to switch to a newer, more convoluted scheme.

The uncertain investor knows that the market is unpredictable, rare things happen regularly, historic highs are hit and then historic lows, atypical patterns are typical. The certain investor knows what will happen, and when it doesn't, he is willing to attribute its failure to some remotely proximate cause, such as "Asian contagion," or "market correction" or "the president or the SEC or some rich old fuck said…"

The uncertain superior investor knows that he might lose, that he is taking a risk. Therefore, he protects himself ahead of time by deciding at what points to get in and out, hedging his bet, stopping his loss, doing what is necessary to protect himself from catastrophic loss. The certain investor knows that he is right, so there's no need to think about being wrong. Consequently, he doesn't have a plan when his investment begins to lose. And so, he acts emotionally. Selling out of fear or buying to prove he's right.

Fear Of Missing Out

Beyond fear of markets, of money, and of uncertainty is FOMO, fear of missing out. This is often seen as just greed, but it isn't. The market can handle greed. In fact, the market requires it. Greed is fairly rational and predictable. Greed looks for the most efficient way. But fear reacts emotionally, impulsively. You should be greedy, but you should never fear that you are missing out. Otherwise, you will always be in fear, since you are always missing out on something somewhere.

Narcissism

Although we tend to see narcissism as a purely psychological issue, it is as physiological as any emotion. Think of the physical reaction you feel when a police officer points and says "you." When the monkey heard the stirring in the bushes, his first thought was, "It's after ME." It takes a cool, rational being to consider all the possibilities that have nothing to do with me.

I don't blame you for being a narcissist. Everybody is born a narcissist and, in our culture, most of us remain one. You are constantly surrounded by the message that you must be extraordinary and unique. Every ad tells you that you're special. "You are so very, very special," every celebrity says. Every movie tells you that just by being yourself, you become extraordinary. Because you are so special and extraordinary, you must have the most unique and self-fulfilling hobby, the most fascinating vacation, the extra-special evening out, the most unique car, the most extraordinary house, the most expensive hi-tech toilet, because even your shit is special. You deserve it just for being you.

These things don't really make you happy, do they? You end up chasing a delusion because—here's the news flash—you aren't that special. You aren't that unique. You don't deserve it just because you're you. And if you think you do, you are setting yourself up to be extraordinarily unhappy. You will feel that you are entitled to everything you want, just because you are you. And if you don't get them, if your dreams are denied, it's an attack on your very identity. Every inconvenience will be seen as a personal insult, every difficulty is an injustice, any skepticism is a betrayal. Your entire life will be filled with anger and resentment, and everything you *do have* will turn to dust and ashes in your mouth.

Anchoring

If you look at how much you have made or lost to help you decide whether to sell an investment, you are engaging in narcissism. Your decision to sell an investment should depend on what current conditions predict will happen in the future. It's got nothing to do with you. Zip, zilch, nada, nuttin, zero. Whether you made or lost money has nothing to do with the future of that stock and therefore should be irrelevant to your decision to sell.

Sometimes it makes good tax sense to know what your profit and loss could be. That taxable effect should be the only consideration. Instead people hang on to bad investments because they don't like to have a loss. That is narcissism. Everyone knows that their past profit or loss has nothing to do with the future value of the investment. And yet they let it affect their decision.

It is such a prevalent occurrence that the behavioral psychologists have a name for it: **anchoring**. The price paid becomes an anchor and you base your expectations on that fixed point. Whatever enormous changes happen in the economic environment, we count that original price paid as our benchmark from which we measure our success or failure. This is a predictable, scientifically verified, psychological mistake. Except for tax purposes, you shouldn't even look at the price you paid. And yet the temptation is great. The superior investor must learn how to resist.

Never Wrong

Behind anchoring is an even more general narcissism. We don't like to be wrong. That's a problem because engaging in uncertain, risky pursuits always means you are going to be wrong at some time and probably more often than you expect. Being wrong is an inevitable part of investing. It doesn't mean you are incompetent or even unlucky. It simply means that you are trying to predict an unknowable future.

An emotional reaction to a loss means that you have not truly accepted the idea of risk and uncertainty. You are still expecting the market to do exactly as you predicted, and you feel emotional pain when you are wrong. Research has shown that this emotional reaction to loss stays with us longer and more powerfully than an emotional reaction to gain. The average-asshole investor is overly influenced by his losses.

The superior investor knows that he is going to be wrong and he is always ready to learn from the error. The loss is taken as a data point in evaluating a strategy. The average investor fluctuates between two reactions. A denial of the loss by refusing to sell the bad investment and making the loss real; or an immediate and emotional rejection of the previous strategy. Both of these result in subpar returns. Refusing to sell a loss means that you are not putting your money to work in a more profitable investment. Emotional changes in strategy almost always means that you sell low what you bought under the old strategy and buy high in your new investments. There are certainly times when you want to keep your losses and when you want to change your strategy, but these should be calm, emotionless decisions based on the market and your tax situation and not on your feelings of emotional pain.

Almost everybody who invests has fallen victim to the mistake of not selling their losses. It feels like the only thing worse than losing money on paper would be to sell the investment and lose the money for real. Retired investors are particularly prone to this mistake, because they fear that they can't recover from any loss. The superior investor knows to sell the bad investment, take the loss and move on.

To make things worse, some fall prey to the temptation to double down on a bad investment. Since they cannot bear the thought of being wrong, they convince themselves that they are right, just not yet. By investing more money in a losing bet, they reason, they are guaranteed to come out ahead. This was just the kind of thinking that led to the collapse of Barings Bank, one of UK's most prestigious establishments, in 1995. A trader at the bank made a mistake on a transaction with Japanese stocks which he hoped to make good on by doubling down. Unfortunately, Japan suffered a massive earthquake and the investment lost even more. What did he do? He doubled down again and lost on that also. He lost on five successive doubling down, bankrupted the bank and was sentenced to six and a half years in prison. The moral is: If you make a bad investment, just take the loss.

Those who are focused on their losses will never be superior investors. They are always afraid of the emotional pain of being wrong. After a few losses, they become afraid of taking risks and will accept the lowest returns for the safest investments. The superior investor knows that he is engaging in a risky, uncertain bet and that losing is a predictable consequence of this. When he invests, he accepts this fact. He can therefore admit when it isn't working and accept the loss. For the superior investor, a loss is a piece of information to be evaluated in terms of the overall strategy, not an emotional event.

Narcissism comes into play when we win too. The superior investor also sees a gain as just a piece of information to be evaluated in terms of the overall strategy. The average-asshole investor feels the gain as an emotional event. He feels that he's on a winning streak, as though the universe of random events now revolves around him. Risk is no longer seen as a possibility of loss, but only as the possibility of even more profits. When irrational exuberance grips the market, it grips him as well and as the risks go up (along with the prices), he keeps making bigger and bigger bets. But risk is still risk, the possibility of profit **and** loss. Eventually the wheel turns and when the average investor loses, he reacts to it emotionally with all the problems described above now magnified.

Illusion of Control

When the market goes up, we think that we have predicted it or even somehow caused it. When it goes down, we feel that we have failed. We react to the uncertainty of risk with the illusion of control. We like to believe that we are the center of the universe with a god-like power over all things. This makes us feel that life is predictable and safe.

This illusion of control is even at the root of the herd-like behavior of market rallies and selloffs. Nobody buying into a rally or selling into a downturn thinks that they are simply following the herd. Everyone thinks that they are ahead of the crowd, selling before the even worse downturn or buying before it goes sky-high. Everyone is smarter than the herd. As in Lake Wobegon, they are all well above average. Those who buy into the illusion of control, never worry that they might be selling low and buying high simply because they are following the herd. As the crowd in Monty Python's *Life of Brian* all chanted in unison, "We are all individuals." We cannot stand the idea that we are not masters of our own fate and therefore pretend to be in control even as we follow the herd.

Confirmation Bias

All the information that might correct our mistakes is filtered through our narcissism. People distort, rationalize or reject any evidence that does not confirm their own beliefs. Any evidence that we are right in our convictions boosts our narcissism and any evidence that we are wrong is rationalized away. When we research investments, we actively seek out proof that we are right and avoid any hint that we are wrong. Psychologists call this confirmation bias. I call it being a fucking idiot.

Psychological Problems in Investing

You cannot get rid of these emotional reactions. Some people are simply born less emotional and these are some of your best investors, however they are often less happy because of the problem their emotionless reactions pose to their marriage and other relations (as I know too well). Those who are born with the normal human emotions must find other ways to deal with it.

Research has pinpointed the amygdala as the seat of our emotions. MRIs show that it is active when we are afraid. Because of its social importance, much of this research has focused on our reaction to other races. What it shows is that those people who are least racist and those who are most racist show similar activation of the amygdala. The monkey that was afraid of other tribes lived to pass on his genes. And we still have that monkey's initial reaction in us. Our amygdala is racist. Where we see the difference between racists and non-racist is in the latest to evolve part of the brain, the prefrontal cortex. The prefrontal cortex is the part of our brain that reflects on ourselves. It can actively suppress the initial reactions of our amygdala. In our first responses, we are all racists, but some of us learn to control that impulse.

How does the nonracist learn to control their initial response? He waits. He reflects on his own biases. He focuses on the individual in front of him instead of the emotional reaction going on inside. The superior investor uses these same techniques. Don't make investment decisions in a *Blink*, no matter what Malcolm Gladwell may argue. Reflect on your biases, don't deny them. Focus on what is happening in the market instead of your reaction to it.

Just as some people are less emotional, some people are more. Those people can take a lesson from the famous marshmallow test in which young children were given the choice of eating a marshmallow now or waiting and getting two marshmallows. How did those who waited succeed in resisting their initial impulse? The most successful technique was to distract themselves, singing little songs, exploring the inside of your nose, blowing spit bubbles…anything to give the higher areas of the brain time to engage. The more emotional investor should wait and distract themselves and then think about these biases and how they are affecting their investment decisions. Only after that should they look at the market again trying to focus on the data in front of them rather than their reaction to it. This is not an argument to not do anything. The superior investor must not be afraid of buying and selling, of taking risks. I'm just saying that you may need to pause so that the more advanced parts of your brain can compensate for the initial reactions of that monkey.

Most importantly, the superior investor knows that they are not the only monkey in the market. People acting in fearful and narcissistic ways cause prices to depart from their true value in predictable ways. People hold on to losses that they should sell. They avoid uncertainty. They become irrationally exuberant. They buy and sell, not because of market opportunities, but just to feel in control. These are all patterns that you can identify and take advantage of.

The two destroyers of investing, Fear and Narcissism, were also the primary emotions of my wife. She was the poster child for Narcissism. And much of what she did, she did out of fear. I believe this was why she planned on murdering me. What cannot be justified out of such fear and narcissism?

At best, fear and narcissism can lose you money. At worst, they can get you killed.

7: Macro Environment

After examining his own soul (i.e. his psychological fallacies), the superior investor looks at the macro environment. Investments are always a transaction between a specific, individual buyer and a seller, the former thinking the price will go up and the latter not so much, but each and every transaction is impacted by a set of bigger processes and trends that is called the macro environment. This includes such things as global growth, geo-political trading relations, anticipated inflation, the domestic monetary environment, interest rates, Fed policy, the business cycle, politics, corruption and demographic changes. The superior investor designs his portfolio of investments to take maximum profit with minimum risk in a particular macro environment.

We will get to picking specific investments, but in this chapter, we will look at the effect of macro-economic factors. This is not just a preparatory step to the real thing. The macro environment causes between 40% and 90% of the movement in any particular investment and, in many ways, it is more predictable than any of the other forces that can cause a price to move. You have to let go of the notion that the price of a stock is determined by what the particular company does or does not do. The performance of the company is only one of the forces affecting its stock price.

We live and invest in a global economic environment which means that the success of our investments can be determined by a Greek bank failure, a slowdown in Chinese manufacturing, a riot in Venezuela or currency swings in Vietnam. We can try to understand and profit from this global environment or we can throw up our hands and put all our money under a mattress, but we cannot change the macro environment or demand a new one. It's like my wife, I could have begged her to change all I wanted, but it was never going to happen.

In this chapter, I will give you the tools to develop your view of the macro environment. This will help you decide the kind of assets that you should invest in: domestic or international, stocks or bonds, commodities or technologies. More importantly, an understanding of the macro environment will protect you from the fear and panic that drives the market after the foreign bank failure or the international currency swing. The average investor does not have this larger view and is surprised by such distant effects. Surprise leads to fear and fear leads to bad investment decisions, as we saw in the last chapter.

Predicting the Market

We will go through a number of macro forces, but you will be trying to decide whether your current macro environment will develop into one of four kinds of markets: 1) early trending up; 2) late trending up; 3) volatile; or 4) a downturn. If it doesn't fit any of these four, we will call it 5) an all-weather market, which means we don't know what the hell is going to happen.

The identification of the type of market will be the most profitable prediction that the investor can make, if correct. Anticipating the macro environment is more consistently profitable than being able to pick the next hot stock. And most individual investors (especially those who follow the news) are better at predicting the macro environment than are short-sighted, market-focused Wall Street professionals. So, the macro is your edge.

Many things about the future are risky, but perhaps the riskiest is making predictions. You've seen the disclaimer many times, "Past results are not necessarily indicative of future performance." Since we are not Delphic oracles, we are prone to get it wrong. Therefore, the superior investor will never put all his money on his prediction. As we start to make predictions, and learn from them, and become better at them, we can make more aggressive investments decisions. But no matter how proficient our forecasts, the superior investor never loses sight of the fundamental uncertainty of risk.

Predictions about future market direction, inflation, fed policy and the like are frequently made by economic pundits. You must ignore all of those. The media showers attention on those pundits who make extreme and pseudo-confident predictions. A recent study of economic pundits looked at what attributes gained the most followers. They found that those pundits who confidently broadcast their predictions had many times the followers of those who were simply correct. And the research showed that as economic pundits became more popular, they also became less accurate in their predictions. I know all the top pundits. I've had dinner with them and discussed investments with them. They are, without exception, idiots. Take my word for it. You would do better to base your investment decisions on fortune tellers than on pundits.

To make your own predictions, you must seek out the quieter experts. Every mutual fund company has economic experts working for them and they regularly communicate their forecasts to their clients. Many companies post these insights for anyone who seeks them out. In forming my own predictions, I regularly read Schwab, Fidelity, Vanguard, Deutsche Bank and T. Rowe Price. All of these can be found on the web for free, although that may change. If you can't get the advice you need for free, you can just invest a couple thousand dollars into the company's funds to get access to their research. If the fund is a good investment anyway, you are getting the research for free.

To be a superior investor, you must form a prediction about the future of the market. Like everything about the future, your prediction is uncertain. You can only predict what is likely to happen. No one can predict what will actually happen. Superior investors position their portfolio to take advantage of what is likely while hedging their bets for what is less likely. They move quickly when they are wrong and try to understand what they may have missed. Average-asshole investors are sure about their prediction and will find others to blame when they are wrong. They therefore never get better at predicting.

Let's go through the main factors affecting the macro one by one and then in the next chapter, we will put them together to illustrate how they combine to form one of five kinds of macro-environments: 1) early trending up; 2) late trending up; 3) volatile; 4) a downturn; or 5) all-weather.

Inflation

The future rate of inflation is one of the most important factors that will affect the success of your investments. Recently, we have been hovering around 2% inflation. It doesn't seem like much, but if you need $80,000 a year to live on now, you'll need almost $120,000 in twenty years to have the same standard of living. Over that twenty years, you will spend $200,000 more than if there were no inflation. And if inflation creeps up to 3%, as many expect, you'll spend $700,000 more over twenty years. And that doesn't count medical, which has been increasing at about 8% per year.

If you believe that inflation will increase, you will make very different investments than if inflation stays low. In times of increasing inflation, most investments in fixed income, such as bonds and certificates of deposit (CD), will actually lose money. If a 1 year CD pays 2% interest and the inflation rate is 3%, you will have lost 1% of your buying power in return for losing access to your money for a year. That's called a lose/lose. Investors seeking protection from inflation must look beyond fixed income investments.

Monetary Policy

Although the inflation rate is often talked about as though it were a force of nature ("The forecast is for rain tomorrow and rising inflation"), it is really a political policy. For thousands of years, there was no inflation to speak of. Indeed, the bigger problem was deflation. Since the amount of money in circulation was tied to a scarce commodity (e.g. gold), the money supply could not keep up with the increased productivity of modern economies. A static amount of money (gold) and an increasing amount of goods (industrial production) means deflation. To solve this problem, developed economies moved away from the gold standard and instituted *fiat* currency where the amount of money can grow and its value is backed by the government that issues it rather than gold.

The problem with a fiat currency is that it is always better for the current political leaders to increase the amount of money in circulation. In the short term, more money makes it easier for businesses and governments to pay off debt and to finance things like social security, Medicare, wars and tax cuts. However, more money increases the chance of uncontrolled inflation which tends to become hyperinflation as workers demand higher wages to be able to afford the higher prices, which now have to be even higher to make up for the increase in wages, and on and on in an ever-increasing cycle.

To keep inflation down, you have to do things that are bad in the short run, but good in the long run., Can you see our current political leaders doing what's good for the long term at the expense of their short-term interests?

To combat this political tendency to hyperinflation, most countries have instituted a central bank (called the Federal Reserve in the U.S.) which is supposed to set policy free from political influence. As I write this chapter, that freedom from political influence seems to be dangerously deteriorating in the U.S. Economists predict that this will mean a short-term spur to the economy, but long-term harm. And since an apolitical Fed is the institution that we rely on to get us out of a broken economy, this long-term harm may be irreparable.

The Federal Reserve Board has the dual mandate of combatting inflation while keeping unemployment low. These are generally seen as conflicting goals since the main way in which inflation is kept down is by increasing unemployment. The primary tool that the Fed has to achieve its goals is to increase or decrease interest rates. Increasing interest rates should slow the economy and put people out of work making them more amenable to lower wages and less able to buy expensive products; thereby controlling prices. A few hundred thousand of mostly young workers losing their jobs seems to be a fair trade for keeping inflation away, at least to those who aren't young and out of work.

Young, working people prefer low interest rates because they are borrowing money to buy houses, start businesses, send their kids to college, etc. And they don't mind inflation just so long as their wages keep rising with the cost of living. Retired people hate inflation and low interest rates. Our wages aren't going up with inflation and low interest rates means we get next to nothing in safe investments like CD's and Treasury bonds. How much longer will retired voters put up with low interest rates? This is another area where we can expect to see political conflict between the generations.

Interest Rates

Interest rates are the primary way that the Federal Reserve Board responds to anticipated inflation. If they think inflation is going to be high, they will raise interest rates. If they think inflation will be low, they will lower interest rates.

Interest rates inversely affect bond prices. When interest rates go up, bond prices go down. To make matters worse, it is not uncommon for interest rates to go down when inflation is already higher than the rate that bonds are paying. For example, in 2012, the rate on a 10-year treasury went below 1.5% for the first time in history while inflation was at 2.1%, meaning that the conservative investor would lose the value of their investment to inflation if everything stayed the same. However, things did not stay the same since the Federal Reserve soon raised interest rates to control inflation which meant that the bond prices went down. Between the loss of value due to inflation and the decrease in bond prices, everyone with Treasuries saw the value of their investment decrease by more than 10% over the next few years. And this is considered to be one of the safest investments for a retired person.

Bonds are not the only investment affected by interest rates. When interest rates are high, stock prices tend to decline. Why put your money in riskier stocks if you can get a decent return on the safer bonds? Also, high interest rates tend to slow the economy since it is more difficult for companies to borrow and invest in the growth of their business. A slow economy means lower profits and therefore declining stock prices.

Even when an economy is growing and strong, increasing interest rates will have a negative effect on stock prices. In fact, they are intended to have that effect. When the economy is heating up, unemployment is low, money is plentiful and inflation is picking up steam, the Federal Reserve is supposed to step in to "take away the punchbowl" by increasing interest rates. The Federal Reserve is supposed to slow the economy in times of prosperity to keep inflation under control and to stimulate the economy during slowdowns to keep unemployment under control. Note that I say under control rather than eliminated, since modern economists believe that some inflation and some unemployment is good for the economy.

Economic Cycles

Politicians want the economy to grow, corporations want to borrow money at the cheapest rate, workers want high paying jobs and consumers want to buy as much as possible. This causes stock prices to rise and dividends to increase. But history has taught us that this also creates inflation. Therefore, the Federal Reserve steps in to slow the economy sending the market down. This up and down creates a dependable cycle for investors to take advantage of.

Cycles are commonly divided into four stages:

Early-Cycle: Being a cycle, we could start at any point. It makes intuitive sense to start the discussion with the early cycle, but one must remember that this comes after the last stage we will discuss, recession. To combat a recession, the Federal Reserve has lowered interest rates to stimulate the economy, credit is easy to get, companies assume that unemployment will soon go down creating more customers with more money to spend.

This is predictably the best time for stocks, which see an average of 25% increase. It is not a good time to be in safe bonds or even cash. This stage usually lasts about a year.

Mid-Cycle: This is typically the longest stage of the economic cycle, lasting an average of three years. It is characterized by continuing, but more moderate growth. Interest rates are still set to encourage growth, but will move to a more neutral rate as the cycle continues. The growth of the most future-oriented companies has tended to slow down, but more conservative companies have joined the party now that they are sure that the economic environment is favorable.

Bonds and cash are still a poor investment, although less so, and stocks are still good, although the rate of growth is usually more moderate. This stage also has the most corrections, with stocks just suddenly dipping 10% for no apparent reason.

Late-Cycle: As the economy continues to grow and inflation builds, the Federal Reserve begins to take away the punch bowl. Workers still have jobs and consumers have money to spend, but it is costing more for companies to borrow and therefore grow their business.

The growth in stocks prices slows and even stalls. The yield on new bonds increases, bringing prices on bonds down, but they become a good buy toward the end of the cycle. Bonds bought right before a recession are one of the best, safest investments you can make. This cycle usually lasts a year and a half with the economy poised to slip into recession.

Recession: The recession phase is usually the shortest, lasting about 9 months. Economic growth stalls and contracts. If they have the political resolve, politicians should be enacting fiscal stimulus. The Federal Reserve lowers interest rates, even though business leaders, politicians and investors will inevitably complain that they aren't doing enough.

Investors will do very well if they sell all their stocks and buy Treasury bonds right before the recession. Once in the recession, stocks do very poorly and bonds outperform. Investors will do equally well if they buy stocks and sell bonds at the very bottom of the recession. That is called market-timing and is notoriously difficult to pull off.

Market Sentiment

In addition to the economic cycle, there is usually a correlate cycle in market sentiment. Market sentiment swings between euphoria and abject fear, between the yearning to buy and the panic to sell. Generally, it is easier for the superior investor to make money out of changes in the market sentiment than in the economic cycle per se. The key to this cycle is investor psychology. The way that investors are viewing risk and uncertainty is of fundamental importance.

Market sentiment is what an economist calls a contrary indicator. A high market sentiment predicts a declining economy sometime soon. A famous story about Joseph Kennedy illustrates the point. In 1929, when Kennedy was offered a stock tip by his shoe shine boy, he sold everything and avoided the great depression. After all, if your shoe shine boy is in the stock market, who else was left to buy and push prices higher?

Market sentiment swings through over-valuing what is already over-valued and then, in reaction to its previous euphoria, overshoots to the downside and prices collapse. Such movements are bound to produce expensive stocks reaching higher prices followed in the cycle by a mixture of failing and undervalued stocks. Thus being aware of market sentiment is vital for the superior investor.

There comes a time when the economy has been in a period of prosperity. Money has been freely lent. Every voice proclaims a bright future. Stock prices continue to go up despite numerous predictions of their decline and every investment is a good investment. The music seems as if it will go on forever, so you keep dancing. You know that stocks are more expensive than ever before, and that only makes you want to invest more. You can always rationalize why it should go even higher. You regretfully add up all the money you've lost because you weren't invested 100% in the hottest stock. Risk looks like your friend, since the more risk you take, the greater the return.

This is the most dangerous time for the retired investor. It is prone to sudden, unpredictable corrections and even recessions. The good times can keep rolling for years or even a decade, but in the space of a few days, it can totally collapse. If someone is investing for far in the future, I would say leave the money in and go for the ride. If (when) we enter a real recession, a young person can tighten the belt like all their friends are doing, try to save more and recover before he needs the money. For the retired person, that is rarely true. You have to be more conservative in your losses. That means that retired investors must have enough money in bonds and cash to endure the coming recession no matter when it comes. Consequently, you will lose some profit in a time when everyone else seems to be making money and prices are setting new records. Since this time is the riskiest for the retired investor, it is when you should invest most conservatively.

Maybe, the sunshine will last forever. The old-fashioned, passé weather pattern where some days are rainy might have changed. This time, it could truly be different. But that's not the way that the superior investor will bet.

The best time to invest is when the market sentiment has plummeted. People become averse to risk. They therefore prefer the most risk-free investments and demand the highest premium for the risk they do take. Companies that had been loaned cheap money in the good times are going out of business, but for the companies that survive, prices are bargains. While the superior investor was pessimistic when everyone else was optimistic, he is now an optimist among pessimists.

Market sentiment is harder to measure, but I would argue it is easier to predict. The key is to recognize its fundamentally psychological nature. The superior investor is able to assess the general psychological state of investors because he follows economic news and is himself one of the data points that make up market sentiment. He should ask himself what he sees in the news, are investors optimistic or pessimistic? Is money flowing in or out? Are investors demanding high premiums for taking risks, or are they seeking out more and more risks in every nook and cranny? Is every dip seen as an investment opportunity, or do they think that the vultures have come home to roost at last? Being able to read market sentiment is the best way for the retired investor to avoid unnecessary risks and make the most profit.

Politics

The capitalist market is not free. It is not a force of nature. It never has been. The capitalist market is a political creation. It is built from laws and regulations. It is a human invention. It always has been. It has predictable human flaws and problems that require government controls and interventions. It always has and always will. A working capitalist economy depends on the laws and regulations of the government and requires occasional government intervention. No student of economic history could possibly believe otherwise. Our economic system depends on a rational and predictable government.

The direction of our political system and its effect on the economy are becoming unpredictable. Inequality is increasing. The number of people who no longer see themselves as part of the American dream is increasing. Resentment and fear are in the driver's seat. Who could have predicted that Donald Trump would be the Republican candidate, let alone our president? Next, like a car overcompensating in a spin, we will veer, unpredictably, the other way. If the Democrats win, we are likely to see open borders, the creation of a universal health care system with no plans to pay for it and the reversal of every policy that Trump reversed of Obama's policies, except of course, continuing to increase the debt. How could economic leaders possibly make rational decisions about investments when they know that the regulations, policies, incentives, and trade relations are likely to reverse with each new election? Rather than investing, doesn't it make more sense in this political climate to just buy back shares and boost the stock price that your salary is tied to?

There is something like a market sentiment in investor's reaction to political events. Everyone knows that the government must be relied on to intervene to fix old and new problems in the capitalist market. Everyone knows that we have the most politicized, interventionist Federal Reserve board in history. And yet investors seem to act as if politics doesn't matter. The superior investor must weigh the political situation along with the other macro factors. Imagine what would happen in our current political divisiveness if we had another 2008-like crises. Do you imagine that the current government could bail out the big banks? Could we institute new, experimental policies like Quantitative Easing? Or what if we have a terrorist attack like 9/11? Would we pull together to reinvigorate the economy or would we fall apart into divisive arguments about who's to blame? Or what if economic growth slows, as most economists predict? We are predicting trillion-dollar deficits with the optimistic forecast of 3% growth, what would the deficit balloon to if there were only 2% growth, or if we fall into recession and have negative growth? Can you imagine our politicians taking the unpopular steps of raising interest rates and cutting spending in the midst of stagflation as was done in the early 80s?

For the conservative investor, the political situation will always matter, but it is hard to imagine a time when it matters more than today. The fact that average-asshole investors are ignoring the political situation makes it even more relevant to the superior investor. This is another example of market sentiment as a contrary indicator. The more that the market seems to ignore the risks of politics, the more dangerous the risks become and the more conservative the superior investor will be.

Corruption

Any time humans are involved, there is always some corruption. It is just in our nature to figure out a way to bend the rules for our own profit. However, corruption wanes and waxes in fairly predictable patterns. You can see large differences in the amount of corruption in different countries. Transparency International (www.transparency.org) calculates an index of the corruption in various countries. Most emerging markets are highly corrupt while many developed are less so, especially, the Scandinavian countries. These make a difference in how you invest. Emerging markets are perennially predicted to show high growth and therefore high profits might be expected for the investor. However, these profits often evaporate through corruption and the investor sees little return for the high risks that they take.

In developed countries, such as our own, corruption is cyclical. During a recession, investors and lenders are much more cautious and tend to root out and eliminate corrupt businesses. During boom times when market sentiment is up and interest rates are down, investors and lenders are much less cautious and so corruption sprouts and grows like fungii on a rotting pile of shit.

Also, as inequality increases, so does corruption. As the rich get richer, they don't just control more money, they also control more political power and therefore the laws and their enforcement. When that happens, corruption becomes legal. You don't need to look any further than the 2008 economic meltdown to see this.

In the years before 2008, most people's mortgages were securitized. That means they were grouped into large pools of mortgages based upon their credit-worthiness. This allowed people to invest in only the most creditworthy mortgages for little interest or high-risk mortgages for more yield. This worked so well that more and more people were able to get mortgages and banks and other lenders were making money hand over fist. However, some banks created a way to make even more money. They saw to it that less creditworthy loans were slipped into the pool of the safest mortgages and then they made bets (called derivatives) that the pool of loans would fail. Those failing loans set off a chain reaction that nearly destroyed our economy.

Was this illegal? Well the financiers that put together the loans defrauded the investors. The banks that knew about this collaborated in the fraud. The credit rating agencies that rated the loans didn't do their legally mandated jobs. But was it illegal? Apparently not. After the savings and loans meltdown of the 1980s, over 1000 people went to jail. After the Nasdaq meltdown, the executives of Enron, Qwest, Tyco and others went to jail. But after the much worse 2008 meltdown, none of the people involved went to jail. Only one bank executive was incarcerated, but that was for hiding how much his bank had lost in the meltdown. Instead, banks were fined, which meant that the investors, like you and me, were punished for what the bank executive did. And the Justice Department officials who were supposed to be prosecuting these crimes? Both Eric Holder, the Attorney General, and Lanny Breuer, head of the investigations, returned to their old firm, Covington & Burling, at much higher salaries where they could further help the law firm's clients, Bank of America, Citigroup and Wells Fargo.

Demographics

For a society, demographics can be destiny. We are currently undergoing a number of demographic changes that will have a crucial effect on the economy and investing. I will briefly describe three of them and how their combined forces are likely to affect the economy.

The first is the wave of births that followed the end of the Depression and World War II which we call the Baby Boom. Second is increased longevity which is starting to level off in developed countries but is still increasing globally. Finally, there is a global decrease in the fertility rate first in the developed countries and increasingly in emerging economies.

The three demographic changes combine to form powerful trends that have and will affect the economy. The baby boomers make up less than 30% of the population, but they control almost 50% of the economy and that number continues to increase. They are used to the mainstream culture reflecting and catering to their needs. As they get older (and because of increased longevity, they will get older than any generation before them), they will expect their society to take care of them. They will demand that, at the very least, our society fulfill those promises that were made to them, such as a fully-funded Social Security and Medicare.

However, the third demographic trend, the decrease in fertility, makes fully funding Social Security and Medicare very difficult, if not impossible. The number of workers whose taxes will fund Social Security and Medicare for this large and increasingly old generation is dwindling. This will shake up our politics, at best, and destroy our economy, at worst.

These trends will also have an effect on interest rates. Older people are savers while younger people are borrowers for college educations, mortgages and credit card debt. The number of savers will increase while the number of borrowers will decrease. This will tend to keep interest rates down, especially for those very safe, income producing investments such as treasury bonds.

****

These are the main macro forces affecting the market. They interact with each other in realtime. They are constantly changing. You have to look for trends, countertrends and feedback mechanisms. It is not a science. No investor is ever scientific. There is no science to the market. There are only interpretations. But that doesn't mean that there aren't good interpretations and bad interpretations. Good interpretations will guide you toward making more money with less risk. Bad interpretations could either ruin you or teach you an important lesson that you'll never forget.

Part Two: What to Invest in Each Market

8: Read This

This section is the meat and potatoes of this book (or if a millennial has read this far, the toast and avocado). You will use this chapter to decide what kind of market we are in now. After that decision you will go to the appropriate chapter where I will provide recommendations for your investments. For example, if you determine that we are in Early Trending Up, you will go to the Early Trending Up chapter to tell you what investments best fit that particular market.

Most of the financial advice you will get from advisors, pundits or investment books is of the buy-and-hold variety. They assume that the average investor cannot understand the macro forces that shape the market and that if the investor engages in trading, they will fall prey to the psychological flaws we've described in Chapter 7. When you were pursuing your career and had little time to understand the market, buy-and-hold was probably the best course. But that is not how the financial professionals invest. Professional investors are always trying to time the market and usually make trades daily. But, of course, the bastards think they're better than us. However, the fact of the matter is that they're not.

The MBA pricks are worse than you at predicting the course of the economy because their focus is on short-term profits and the latest economic headline. If you follow the news and have a broad perspective, you are likely to have a better understanding of the macro-forces that affect the economy. In fact, understanding broader, long-term trends is our edge over the professional traders.

This book gives you the tools to determine the kind of market we are in now. And once you've determined the kind of market, I will tell you what to invest in. When the kind of market changes, you will turn to another chapter, sell some of your investments and buy new ones.

Determining the kind of market is the most profitable investing decision you will make. If you take your time and can understand the factors described in the last chapter, you will do better at this than any of those MBA assholes and ivy league pricks. With this knowledge, you will get and stay wealthy in retirement.

Five Kinds of Markets

Inflation, monetary policy, interest rates, economic cycles, market sentiment, politics, corruption, and demographics. As described in the last chapter, these are the factors that you should analyze in order to predict what the economy will do. For investing, it is useful to formulate your prediction as one of five types of markets:

1) Early Trending Up; 2) Late Trending Up; 3) Volatile; 4) Downturn; or 5) All-weather Market. I will briefly describe the type of investments that you should make in each type of market and then discuss the likelihood of such a market in the near future, as I see it at the time I am writing this.

Early Trending Up

This market is usually in the early part of an economic cycle. It will have low inflation, loose monetary policy and low interest rates. Corruption will be low. Market sentiment will be rising, but still cautious. Equities in these type of markets have typically produced a 20% return.

This is the best time to be in stocks. The equities that tend to do the best are technology, industrials, financials and discretionary consumables. Companies that are willing to borrow money to grow do especially well. Telecommunication and utility stocks tend to lag the market. You should avoid bonds except as insurance against a sudden downturn.

It is highly unlikely that we will see this market anytime soon. It has been almost 10 years since the start of the economic up cycle. The Fed and politicians have instituted policies that have goosed the market and given us low inflation, loose monetary policy and low interest rates, but this is unlikely to have any further effect.

Late Trending Up

In this market, inflation is rising and, in response, we can expect that interest rates are or will soon be rising with monetary policy becoming restrictive. Market sentiment is stronger than is warranted by the actual performance of the companies. Stock market highs are often reached producing headlines, but the actual return on investment is relatively small. This is the time when corruption tends to be highest although it may not be discovered until a downturn.

This is when the superior investor should start to take profits and move into cash. Because of this, the superior investor will lag the market. Consequently, this market makes the greatest demand on the investor's discipline as fear of missing out takes hold. This is not a good time to buy growth stocks with high debt or to look for new value stocks. Energy, commodities and material sectors usually do well, at least keeping up with increasing inflation. Defensive equities, such as consumer staples and health care can also do well and it is a good time to look for large cap stocks that have provided steady dividends. All of these should still do fairly well when the inevitable recession hits.

This market type is what we are entering as I write this chapter. This phase typically lasts a year and a half, but because of the low inflation and the artificially long early-trending-up market, it is difficult to predict. The demographics of baby boomers retiring will tend to keep interest rates low because many retired people prefer to have bonds no matter how low the interest rate. High inflation may yet rear its ugly head causing the fed to raise interest rates that could send us immediately into recession or the revelation of systemic corruption could cause us to entirely skip over this late-trending-up market. Because of the unusual circumstances of our time, the Fed-goosed economy, lack of political stability and increasing systemic corruption, the superior investor should be even more conservative than usual.

Volatile

Inflation is usually moderate, monetary policy is neutral and interest rates may be slowly rising. Market sentiment is volatile and tends to overreact to both good and bad news. Politics is usually highly relevant with off-hand remarks of economic and political leaders having significant but temporary effects.

This is still a good time to be in equities which usually return 5 to 7%, although with many ups and downs along the way. Typically, no sector will lead consistently, so this is a good time to be invested in broad index funds that focus on minimum volatility both in the U.S. and in the more stable foreign countries with little corruption. It is also a good time to look for value stocks that you can buy during a correction, especially quality, large-cap companies.

The greatest danger in this type of market is that a short-term correction will turn into a major downturn. Since the investor is likely to buy more equities on the way down and to have few treasuries, a sudden major downturn can be catastrophic. The conservative investor should always keep this in mind and have enough in reserve to survive a major downturn.

As I write this chapter, there are some indications that we may soon enter a Volatile Market, but we are not there yet.

Downturn

Inflation is down and deflation may be threatening. The fed is lowering interest rates and monetary policy is expansionary to try to stimulate the economy. Market sentiment is strongly negative. Politicians are prone to overreact and push for less imports, negative interest rates and quantitative easing that could make the downturn worse. This is the time when corruption is most likely to be uncovered.

Downturns provide some of the best opportunities for investors, although it requires more than a little luck to fully take advantage of them. Right before the downturn is the best time to buy bonds. Right at the bottom of the downturn is the best time to buy stocks. Being a bit late on buying bonds or a bit early for buying stocks doesn't lose you that much.

We seem to be entering a period of slow growth in a late cycle. However, this could easily turn into a recession that may be very difficult to pull out of. Recessions can happen because of widespread corruption or geopolitical and trade risks and these are a growing danger in the current environment. More often, recessions have been caused by people dealing with investments or macro environments that are more complex than they understand. Today we are undoubtedly in that kind of environment:

- The global trading system with its just-in-time inventories, flexible supply chains and floating currencies is a completely new system that dominates the global economy and squeezes out all alternatives. No one

- could possibly claim to understand what vulnerabilities it contains nor could anyone estimate how far-flung it's damage might be.
- We seem to have entered a time of perennially low-inflation. Many pundits claim to have theories about why this has happened, but I note that none of them predicted it before it happened, and all of the theories seem to have the same premise, which is, "this time is different." Any sudden change in the inflation rate would have catastrophic consequences. The federal reserve has created a monetary environment that depends on low inflation. If inflation increases—as all economic theories before our current low inflation predicted—our deficit spending, debt-increasing government would make it very difficult to bring inflation under control. Indeed, the feds would need to quickly and precipitously raise interest rates. The resulting increase in unemployment, cut back on spending and run-away interest on the national debt would be guaranteed to make the political system even more unstable. Whatever would happen next cannot be good.
- None of the systemic problems that led to the 2008 meltdown have been fixed (mortgages are still securitized in the same way with the same vulnerabilities). The only difference is that the watchdogs have been watching very closely. How much longer you think that can continue depends on your belief in the efficacy of bureaucrats to get the job done when the safety of the market is in direct contradiction to the goals of their political bosses.

I have not considered a number of macro forces that could be catastrophic although they are off everyone's radar. What would happen if major financial systems were hacked? What if a new "me-too" movement focuses on economic crimes, such as exploitation and wage-slaves? What if a Democrat is elected who opens our borders to all? What if Trump is re-elected and he replaces all the fed members with his puppets? What if global warming surges much more quickly than anticipated? What if there's a nuclear war?

The greatest danger is that we will have a downturn that will last longer than your money. In such a situation, you must have a plan B thought out and ready to implement. You should be able to cut your spending down to necessities and you should have fully prepared a way to make money.

All-weather Market

If you can't determine the kind of market we are in, then you should invest in an all-weather portfolio. In this undetermined market, the interest rates could go up, but they also could go down. The economy could speed up or it could slow down. Inflation may accelerate or it could deaccelerate. We just don't know. The all-weather portfolio should protect you against any possibility.

Degree of Likelihood

Of course, all of these scenarios are only possibilities. You should formulate your prediction as a degree of likelihood for each of the four types of markets. You should write down that likelihood and briefly record your reasons for that. It's best to do this every six months. You must review your past predictions, trying to determine what you got wrong or right. As with most things, predicting the market is something you can get better at if you will allow yourself to learn from your mistakes. You should plan to be very conservative in your predictions for at least a year. And you must always be prepared for something catastrophic happening. The market is always uncertain and investing is always risky.

Keeping track of your predictions and rigorously evaluating them is especially important today when the investor is faced with new conditions that have never before been encountered. But don't think that these new conditions mean that we cannot or should not make predictions. Nobody can understand all of the raw economic data without some way of interpreting it. We only know that we are encountering new conditions because they don't fit our old interpretations. Learning means that we recognize the deficiencies of our old predictions, it doesn't mean making no predictions at all.

Don't Go Yet

Take your time determining the kind of market we are in. This is the most important investing decision you will make. This is something you will get better at if you practice the analyses presented in this book. However, you will never get perfect. Only average asshole investors think they are always right. Superior investors are always uncertain. Therefore, superior investors, especially retired ones, must protect themselves when they turn out to be wrong.

There are two ways for the retired investor to protect their investments: Diversification and Cash.

Diversification

If the future were perfectly predictable, we would just put our money into the investments that we knew would be going up. However, we are human and to make matters worse, we are investing in a market that is just the aggregate of the buying and selling decisions of other fallible and irrational humans. Therefore, we must protect our investments because our prediction of what the market is likely to do may not happen until long after it becomes likely.

The superior investor thinks of their portfolio of investments in terms of a return/risk ratio. We are not seeking the highest return but the best return with an acceptable risk. The average asshole thinks only of how much he will make. If tech stocks are setting records and have piled up huge earnings in the recent past, the average investor would like to put all his money into tech stocks. But the superior investor sees record setting prices as an increased risk and he prepares for a future that may differ from the recent past. This is the point of diversification.

You may have heard that diversification is the only free lunch in investing. This is true, but to understand that, you must look at the return/risk ratio of the entire diversified portfolio. To determine the return of a portfolio, you just add up the return of all the investments. But to determine the risk of the portfolio, you don't just add up the risk of all the separate stocks. The free lunch comes from looking at how the risks of different investments are correlated with each other.

For example, the longer the term of a treasury bond, the higher the risk, since many more unpredictable events might happen in the next 20 years than in the next 3 months. Therefore, the return of a long-term bond is higher than a short-term bond to compensate the investor for the added risk. Money invested in an S&P stock ETF is also risky, about as risky as a 20-year bond. The investor who puts money into both will be able to add up the return from the bonds and the stock ETF, but his risk will go down because when the stock ETF goes down, the bond will usually go up, and vice versa. This means that the bond and the stock are not correlated, in fact they are inversely correlated. When the risk of a particular investment is not correlated with the risk of the rest of the portfolio, the overall risk of the portfolio goes down. The free lunch of diversification comes from reducing your expected risk more than you reduce your expected return. In other words, you have a better return-risk ratio.

Not everybody likes to diversify. If you know how to predict the future with accuracy, then you should not diversify. You should invest all of your money into whatever stock the fortune-teller or Ouija board or astrological chart tells you to. Also, if you love the thrill of gambling, of risking it all on one turn of the roulette wheel, then diversification is not for you, but then really, investing isn't for you either. Diversification is for those who believe that learning how to deal with what you don't know is more important than anything you do know.

Diversification is not just a matter of buying a lot of different stocks. You could buy the stock of 100 different companies and still not be diversified if all the companies are in the same sector. Intel, Cisco and Broadcom are all highly correlated, which means that they go up and down together, so you are not reducing your risk by much when you invest in all three. Nevertheless, for some people, this is all of the diversification they are looking for. They are 100% sure that the tech sector will go up and they just want to make sure that they aren't hurt by the idiosyncratic failure of one company. By now you should know that those people are not superior investors because superior investors are never 100% sure of anything.

Most investors look to diversification to get rid of all unsystematic risk, so that they will bear only the risk that the entire market may go down. This is the type of diversification that many ETF's will give you. For example, if you have an S&P 500 ETF, then the failure of one company or the plunge of one sector isn't going to hurt you very much. You will only be badly hurt of the entire market goes down.

We, however, will aim at an even stronger kind of diversification. We want the investments that make up our portfolio to respond differently to changes in the macro economy. Since we will be investing most of our money in the prediction of a particular kind of market—for example, Early Trending Up--we will diversify by choosing some of the investments that will do well if we are wrong. In Early Trending Up markets, stocks do well, so we will put most of our money into stocks. If we are wrong in our prediction of an Early Trending Up market, then bonds will likely do well, so we will put some of our money in bonds to protect against being wrong in our prediction.

This means that we will always do worse than if we put all our money into the correct prediction. If our prediction of Early Trending Up is correct, then the money that we put in bonds will be a drag on our returns. But we will dampen volatility, keeping our returns on a steadier and more predictable course and we will avoid economic catastrophes. If something unpredictable happens to cause an Early Trending Up market to crash, our bonds will still do well. In retirement, avoiding economic catastrophes is more important than getting the highest possible returns. And when you are withdrawing money to live on, less volatility, especially in the early years, means that you'll have a much better chance of making your assets last.

The average asshole will wait for something unexpectedly bad to happen before they diversify. The superior investor will diversify before anything happens. For example, when the stock market crashed in late 2008, the bond market soared. Those who diversified before the crash came out smelling like roses. Those who waited to diversify until the crash began lost their money in stocks as they sold them and lost it again in bonds because they bought in at the height.

You have to diversify as you invest. Then you will get behavioral advantages as well as financial advantages. When you are not diversified and it looks like your expectations are wrong and all of the investments based on that expectation are crashing, then fear tends to take hold. That is when you are most likely to do something stupid. You wouldn't be the first person to bake in all their losses by selling at the bottom and then staying out as the market climbs in the recovery.

Cash

The worst thing in retirement is being forced to withdraw money when the market is down. In order to protect yourself from that, you should have one year of necessary and discretionary spending plus another year of necessary spending in a safe money-equivalent account, such as a money market fund, short-term treasury ETF, a saving account, or a conservative bond fund like Fidelity's FCONX. You should withdraw from this only when the market is down more than 7% and you should replenish this fund when the market goes back up.

People who are working and earning a paycheck generally need to hold less cash than people who are retired and drawing from their portfolios. The virtue of holding cash in retirement is that you're buying yourself protection against having to withdraw from stocks or bonds following a big disruption in either market.

You can arrive at the right amount of cash holdings by looking at the Spreadsheet you created in Chapter four. Look on the row labeled **Withdraw** in the column for next year. Add to that the amount in the row, **Invest Income** also for next year. Or you can calculate your expenditures for the year ahead, then subtract any amounts that you'll receive from guaranteed, nonportfolio sources, such as Social Security or a pension. The amount that's left over is your annual portfolio withdrawal. For example, let's say you expect to spend $80,000 for necessary and discretionary expenses, and you receive $35,000 per year from Social Security. In that instance, you are going to need $45,000 in cash to cover your expenditures. For the second year, you will only need $50,000 to live on because you are going to cut back on discretionary spending (no trips to Italy this year!) and you will still receive $35,000 meaning you'll have to draw $15,000 from your cash for the second year. To cover two years of a recession, you are going to have to have a cash cushion of $45,000 plus $15,000 or $60,000 in cash or a cash equivalent

Some people think they need to be able to access all their retirement savings to deal with emergencies or unforeseen situations — that can be a costly mistake. Most of your money needs to be put to work in investments. The more that you have parked in cash means the less you will have to generate retirement income. Long-term growth will almost certainly have to come from exposing some of your money to risk in stocks, real estate, or your own business (or perhaps all three). It is unlikely that you will be able to accept the uncertainty of these investments without having a base of savings that feels truly safe.

How to Use the Following Chapters

After this chapter, you will only read one of the other chapters in this section. If you determine that the market is Late Trending Up. Then go to the Late Trending Up chapter. Skip over the Early Trending Up, Volatile, Downturn and All-weather chapters. You don't need them now and they will seem repetitious, since I fully explain each investment, even if I have already explained it in an earlier chapter. I assume that you skipped the early chapter to get to the chapter that is about the market you are in now.

So, in this section of the book, you will only read two chapters: this one and the one that corresponds to our current kind of market. When you have read those two chapters, go on to Part 3.

9: Early Trending Up

You are in the right chapter if the market is recovering from a recent downturn or recession and if inflation is low, monetary policy is loose and interest rates are low.

Transition to the new market

Look at the percentages at the end of this section. Take the next six weeks to sell anything you own if it isn't on this list. If you have a bond fund, sell it until it's only 5% of your investment. If you have Value Stocks, sell them. Research has shown that the most efficient way to cash these in is to sell one-fifth of your over-investments every week.

As money frees up, use it to buy your new investments. You can skip two weeks of your choice. Before each buy, take another look at your macro forces to make sure you are in the right market. You should have all your new investments bought in seven weeks.

Determining How Much and Where to Diversify

The goal of investing is to grow your wealth and provide you with income for the rest of your life. However, with growth comes risk and the goal of diversification is to dampen that risk. Risk may be your friend when you're young and have income from working to get you through, but it can be devastating in retirement.

There are 3 risks in an Early Trending Up Market: 1) a sudden unpredicted catastrophe, 2) increasing inflation causing the Fed to tighten monetary policy and 3) a return of whatever caused the last recession. The best protection against these are U.S. Treasury bonds. Whatever your criticism of the U.S. government and its debt, buyers of bonds know that the U.S. is the safest guarantor in the world. Neither cash, nor gold, not bitcoins come close to matching the diversifying power of bonds backed by the full faith of the U.S. government.

Bonds

U.S. bonds usually have one of the lowest yields of any investment, but the importance of bonds is not their yield, but their safety. When equities and other growth investments are plunging, Treasury bonds are rising. When everyone is fleeing to safety, the safety they flee to are U.S. bonds.

You can buy U.S. Treasury bonds directly online at TreasureyDirect.gov. But it is generally easier to buy them as part of an ETF. ETFs are term diversified and usually more liquid, being tradable anytime the stock market is open.

When you buy a bond, you are lending money to the bond seller. The seller might be a corporation, a city, the U.S or a foreign government. Most bonds incur three risks: 1) the borrower declares bankruptcy and you don't get paid back; 2) the borrower pays you off early and so you don't receive all the expected income; and 3) you want to sell the bond early and you can't get what you paid for it. None of these risks are believed to apply to U.S. treasuries.

However, there is a fourth risk that applies to every loan. It is inflation. This means that you'll get the money that you loaned back, but that amount of money won't be worth as much. Inflation alone is not a problem in Early Trending Up, since climbing stocks seem to thrive on inflation. It is only a problem if the Feds decide to restrict the money supply in order to control inflation. In that case bonds will go down, but less than stocks.

Of course, there are many kinds of bonds, but Treasuries are the most defensive. If the market crashes, you will be able to sell your bonds at a profit and then invest them at the bottom and so regain the lion's share of your wealth during the fast upsurge that follows a crash.

Corporate Bonds will pay higher yield than treasuries, but they will provide little protection since they tend to go down when the market goes down. This is especially true of the higher yielding corporate bonds, often called junk bonds. When Treasury yields are down, the average asshole investor will "chase returns" and buy junk bonds to get the higher return that he feels is necessary. This is never a good idea, but especially not in this market. In this Early Up Market, people tend to take on too much risk for too little return, and this is exactly what buying junk bonds does. Junk bonds are priced off of Treasuries. When Treasury yields are down, so are junk bond yields. That means that you are getting less reward for more risk. The successful investor is always looking for more reward for less risk.

It is best to buy a long-term Treasury ETF, since those will give you the most protection. Vanguard's Long-Term Treasury Index Fund ETF (VGLT), SPDR Long Term Treasury ETF (SPTL) and Schwab Long-term US Treasury ETF (SCHQ) all have very low expense ratios.

To Diversify, **5%** of your money in an Early Trending Up Market should be in a long-term Treasury ETF.

Cash

When investors say cash, they don't just mean actual dollar bills. Cash includes money-market funds, cash-management accounts maintained by brokers and short-term Treasuries. The important features are that these have very low volatility and are liquid, i.e. you can get your money out within a day or less.

The most convenient place for the investor to keep cash is in a broker's cash-managed account. These are usually swept every night into FDIC insured bank accounts and they often pay competitive interest rates. However, you must check to be sure that this is true, since some brokers depend on convenience alone to attract your money.

Money market funds and money market accounts are tied to short-term fixed income investments like U.S. Treasuries. They usually pay a bit more than savings accounts and broker cash-managed accounts. Money market *funds* are not FDIC insured against losses, but money market *accounts* are.

Short-term treasuries usually pay a little more than money-markets but they are a bit more volatile and not quite as liquid because you must wait for a buyer before you can access the money. Normally that is not a problem, but it could become a problem during times of extreme stress when you most need to pull the money out.

For Diversification and transitioning into cash, you should put your money into your broker's cash-management funds that pay competitive interest rates and are insured, such as Vanguard Federal Money Market or Fidelity Money Market Fund. If your broker doesn't automatically put your uninvested cash into a Money Market account. Find out how that can be arranged.

<u>5%</u> of the money in an Early Trending Up Market should be in cash.

Exchange Traded Funds (ETFs)

An Early Trending Up market is the best time to be fully invested in stocks since their price is usually comparatively low and, if history is any predictor, they are on their way up. What do I mean by fully invested? It means that the only money that you should have in investments other than stocks is to protect yourself against unpredicted changes.

There are several ways in which you can be invested in stocks. The most popular is a mutual fund, because it is often the only choice in 401(k)s. Although there are a number of good mutual funds, most of them are not suitable for the retired investor. Funds have the advantage of allowing the investor to easily diversify, but they have more fees, less liquidity and often only a false promise of diversity. For example, a popular choice are target date mutual funds that become more conservative in their investment as you age. These are great while you are working and just accumulating money with little thought as to how best to invest it. They are not appropriate for you in retirement. Your first clue should be the target date of the fund, which is supposed to be the year you retire(d). If your fund is called something like Target2015, then it's time to wake up. 2015 is long gone and it ain't coming back.

ETFs are the easiest, most versatile, lowest fee and usually the most tax efficient. They are easiest because they can be traded just like any stock and unlike mutual funds, you never have to pay a broker any load fee, neither a front-end load when you buy it or a back-end load when you sell it. They are more versatile because of the huge, diverse and expanding population of special focus ETFs, as well as the fact that they can be traded anytime the market is open and you don't have to wait until the end of the day to buy or sell.

ETFs have the lowest fees. Just go to any financial website, such as Yahoo.com and compare the expense ratio of an ETF with a mutual fund. Even worse, mutual funds are allowed to collect hidden fees that are not counted in the expense ratio listed on financial sites. These are called 12b-1 fees and they basically allow mutual funds to charge you for the advertising that they have used to get you to buy their product. If this wasn't bad enough, the regulation is never investigated and rarely enforced so that companies can give parties for all their friends, call it market research and have you pay for it.

Finally, ETFs are more tax efficient. Managing your investments for tax efficiency is especially important for the retired investor. Upon retirement, we usually have more money sitting in taxable and non-taxable accounts than ever before. And we depend on that money lasting for the rest of our life. It won't last if we let the government collect high taxes every quarter. In addition, unmanaged taxable income can reduce your social security. ETFs will let you manage your taxes better than mutual funds. Mutual funds must distribute capital gains to the shareholder when a stock in the fund is sold for a profit. So a mutual fund holder will have capital gains whenever the mutual fund decides to sell something, which happens frequently. However, you only pay capital gains on an ETF when you sell the ETF. Therefore, you get to choose when you take capital gains and can do it when it is most tax efficient for you.

One of the best ETFs you can buy is one that owns the S&P 500. The first was SPY by State Street Global Advisors and they are still one of the best, but Vanguard, Fidelity, Blackrock and many others offer the same product. The investor should simply choose the one with the least fees.

At least **40%** of the money that you have invested for Early Trending Up should be in an S&P 500 ETF.

How to Buy an ETF

Buying an ETF is just like buying a stock. Buying and selling stocks and ETFs has gone through tremendous changes in the last decade, many of which are to the advantage of the retired investor. Previously, trading fees could easily eat up the unwary investor's capital, since it was not unusual to pay $100 or more for each trade. Today the individual investor can make trades for free.

The first thing is to make sure that you have a brokerage account--which is free to set up--and then fund it with the money you intend to invest. Once the account is ready, you can initiate a trade.

When you trade in a brokerage account, you will be offered choices about how the trade should be placed. The most common trade is a *limit order*. The investor puts in a maximum price that he is willing to pay for the ETF and the ETF is not bought unless it gets down to that price or below. This means that the trade may not happen if the price does not go down to or below your limit price. The buyer can also allow the limit order to expire at the end of the day or to continue until it is canceled or a number of days (usually 60) has passed. The investor needs to be careful when using Good Till Canceled since they are easy to forget and may make a trade when market conditions have changed so that you no longer wish to buy that ETF.

The buyer also has the choice of a market order which means that the ETF will be bought at the next available price. This is rarely a good idea, especially when the ETF or stock is thinly traded. Opportunistic traders can take advantage of a market order to sell you an ETF at a premium.

Diversifying for Profits

There are two kinds of diversification. What people usually mean by diversification is defensive diversification. That means diversifying in case your assumptions about the economy are wrong. For example, you may think that the economy will be Early Trending Up, but some glitch may happen and it may suddenly be in a Downturn. The superior investor always assumes that they may be wrong and prepares for that possibility by not investing all of their money in the current assumption.

A second kind of diversification is diversifying for profit. Here you choose a mix of the type of investments that will do well in the type of economy that you are assuming--in this case, Early Trending Up. This protects you from an unpredicted failure in one area and should give you as much profit with less risk. Therefore, although an S&P 500 ETF should be your best investment in this market, we will diversify into other investments that promise to do about as well.

Small Cap ETF

The S&P 500 is made up of large and mid-size corporations with very few small corporations. In the Early Trending Up period, small companies do significantly better than larger companies. Small companies usually have more debt than large companies, so low interest rates are especially helpful. Also, small companies are still growing their customer base, so a growing economy with happy, optimistic customers helps small companies grow even faster.

You should have at least **15%** of the money invested for Early Trending Up in a small cap ETF, such as Vanguard's Small-Cap ETF (VB), or iShares Russell 2000 Growth ETF (IWO). If you prefer a mutual fund, there is Vanguard's Tax-Managed Small Cap (VTMSX).

Investing in the World

The S&P 500 only invests in companies that are domiciled in the U.S. However, when U.S. stocks are doing well, the entire world is usually doing well also, and some countries are doing considerably better. Therefore, it is a good idea to have some investments outside the U.S. However, it should be noted that the S&P 500 is already international. Even though the companies are based in the U.S. 30% of the revenue of the S&P 500 companies come from outside the U.S.

To increase the international exposure, the retired investor should have about **7%** of the money invested for Early Trending Up in a Foreign Equity ETF, such as Vanguard's All-World ex-US (VXUS), Fidelity's ZERO International Index Fund (FZILX) or iShares Core EAFE (IEFA).

Sector Momentum Trends

Companies are grouped into sectors with other similar companies. For example, Marathon Oil, Halliburton and Conoco Phillips are all in the Energy sector. This can be further divided into Industries. Marathon Oil and Conoco Phillips are both in the Oil, Gas & Consumable Fuels industry, while Haliburton is in the Energy Equipment & Services Industry. Stocks in the same Industry usually move up or down together. Sectors also tend to move up or down together although they are more diverse.

There are ETFs that target a particular sector. I will list them with their Fidelity ETFs, although there are other investment companies with sector ETFs. There are eleven sectors: Communication Services (FCOM), Consumer

Discretionary (FDIS), Consumer Staples (FSTA), Energy (FENY), Financials (FNCL), Health Care (FHLC), Industrials (FIDU), Information Technology (FTEC), Materials (FMAT), Real Estate (FREL) and Utilities (UTIL).

In an Early Trending Up economy, the following sectors usually do well: Real Estate, Consumer Discretionary, Industrials, Materials, Information Technology and Financials. We will leave Real Estate for another topic.

Create a chart in a charting website. I like PerfChart on StockCharts.com (they try to get you to buy access, but look around the website for the free charts) because it incorporates both the stock's price and its dividends to give a total return. Most other charting websites only show the price. Put in the ETFs for Consumer Discretionary, Industrials, Materials, Information Technology and Financials so that you can see the trend lines since the start of the Late Trending Up period. We are going to compare their Momentum Trends.

Momentum is the tendency of an investment to persist in its trend. If it's going up, it tends to continue to go up, and if it's going down, it goes lower. A momentum strategy tries to take advantage of this tendency in the market. The strategy does not depend on looking at fundamentals or developing your own prediction of what the market will do. You cannot anticipate a trend; you can only identify one. You won't catch the first move higher; you will only jump on board after the train has left the station.

Momentum is sometimes referred to as a factor. There have been a number of factors identified that are supposed to identify market anomalies so that the investor can take advantage of them. Some of the better-known factors are small size, high quality, low volatility and hundreds of others that are less known. Studies have shown that the market does not correctly price the stocks with the factors and suggests that those in the know can take advantage of this.

Unfortunately, these factors tend to disappear once the anomaly is known. For example, after a study has shown that the market underprices low-volatility stocks, investors are willing to pay more for them. The only factor that hasn't disappeared after the anomaly was revealed is momentum. In fact, momentum appears to have increased. If you think about it for a minute, you'll understand why. If people start paying a higher price for low-volatility stocks, then the anomaly disappears and future earnings will be right in line with the price paid. However, if people start to pay higher prices for stocks with momentum, the momentum will increase and push the price even higher increasing the anomaly. Of course, eventually the price will come back to reality, but meantime the momentum strategy pays off handsomely.

Examine the chart you've created that shows the trend of your sectors since the start of the Early Trending Up period. If one or two stand out, invest in those sector ETFs. You should put in about **20%** of your money. If no sector stands out, put the 20% in your S&P 500 ETF. Check your sectors every week while Early Trending Up continues and make adjustments to suit the trends, looking not at the immediate past, but at the trend since the start of the Late Trending Up market.

REITs

Real estate investment trusts, or REITs are real-estate companies. Buying stock in a REIT, earns you a share of the income produced by renting, leasing or selling the real-estate. By law, REITs must pay out at least 90% of their taxable income to shareholders as dividends and most pay out all of it. Because of the constant flow of income, REITs are not very tax efficient and are best held in a non-taxable account.

REITs do consistently well in an Early Trending Up market. Companies are growing and they need more office space, warehouses and other commercial property. At the same time, interest rates—which have an outsized effect on real estate—are down. The investor will get a double payoff: not only will the price of the stock go up, but you will earn a monthly dividend.

8% of the money that you have invested in Early Trending Up should be in a REIT ETF such as Fidelity's FREL, Vanguard's VNQ or Schwab's SCHH.

Rebalancing

As time passes, the vagaries of the market will change your investment allocations. If REITs do really well, they may soon make up more than 8% of your investments. Rebalancing means selling and buying investments to bring you back to your original allocations. This means that you are buying those investments that performed the worst and selling those that performed the best. This may feel anti-intuitive, but research has proven this to be the best strategy. It sounds better if you say that you are buying low and selling high.

In an **Early Trending Up** market, your investments should look like this:

40-60% in an **S&P 500 index ETF**
15% in a **Small-Cap ETF**
7% in a **Foreign Equity ETF**
0-20% in 1 or 2 **Sector ETF**s
8% in a **REIT ETF**
5% in a **Long-term Treasury ETF**
5% in **Cash**

10: Late Trending Up

You are in the right chapter if the economy is strong and it has been for at least a year. Everybody is optimistic that it will continue so there is less and less of a premium for taking risks. However, inflation is starting to rise and we can anticipate that at some time the Fed will take the punch bowl away by beginning to raise interest rates.

Transition to the new market

Look at the percentages at the end of this section. Take the next six weeks to sell anything you own if it isn't on this list. If you have a bond fund, sell it. If you have Value Stocks, sell them. Research has shown that the most efficient way to cash these in is to sell one-fifth of your overinvestments every week. You can skip one week of your choice, and you can double up one week, but it needs to be all sold in 6 weeks.

As money frees up, use it to buy your new investments. You can skip two weeks of your choice. Before each buy, take another look at your macro forces to make sure you are in the right market. You should have all your new investments bought in seven weeks.

Fear of Missing Out

Everybody is making money. Headlines proclaim new market highs. Everyone agrees that this bull market will go on forever. Nobody thinks risk is bad, so they don't demand much of a premium for it. This is the most dangerous time for the retired investor.

In this market, your main job is to prepare for the downturn while still making some profit from the booming economy. However, you must accept the fact that you will not make as much money as others. As the market continues to go up, you will start to feel that you are missing out. This is the time when you must stay disciplined.

When the market is driven by Fear Of Missing Out, the market is at its riskiest. That is when you must start to take some profits off the table.

Determining How Much and Where to Diversify

The goal of investing is to grow your wealth and provide you with income for the rest of your life. However, with growth comes risk and the goal of diversification is to dampen that risk. Risk may be your friend when you're young and have income from working to get you through, but it can be devastating in retirement.

The two greatest risks in a Late Trending Up Market are corruption and increased inflation leading to higher interest rates. These often go together since the falling stock market caused by higher interest rates will reveal corruption. As Warren Buffet said, "Only when the tide goes out do you discover who has been swimming naked." In such cases, the best protection is cash.

As a Late Trending Upward market continues, its susceptibility to corruption increases. So does the likelihood that interest rates will take off. Toward the end of this chapter, we will describe how to increase your defensive diversification as the Late Trending Up gets later.

Cash

When investors say cash, they don't just mean actual dollar bills. Cash includes money-market funds, cash-management accounts maintained by brokers and short-term Treasuries. The important features are that these have very low volatility and are liquid, i.e. you can get your money out within a day or less.

The most convenient place for the investor to keep cash is in a broker's cash-managed account. These are usually swept every night into FDIC insured bank accounts and they often pay competitive interest rates. However, you must check to be sure that this is true, since some brokers depend on convenience alone to attract your money.

Money market funds and money market accounts are tied to short-term fixed income investments like U.S. Treasuries. They usually pay a bit more than savings accounts and broker cash-managed accounts. Money market *funds* are not FDIC insured against losses, but money market *accounts* are.

Short-term treasuries usually pay a little more than money-markets but they are a bit more volatile and not quite as liquid because you must wait for a buyer before you can access the money. Normally that is not a problem, but it could become a problem during times of extreme stress when you most need to pull the money out.

For Diversification and transitioning into cash, you should put your money into your broker's cash-management funds that pay competitive interest rates and are insured, such as Vanguard Federal Money Market or Fidelity Money Market Fund. If your broker doesn't automatically put your uninvested cash into a Money Market account. Find out how that can be arranged.

To Diversify, **10%** of your money in a Late Trending Up Market should be in cash. As described below, you will increase that percentage as the Late Trending Up Market gets older.

Exchange Traded Funds (ETFs)

There are several ways in which you can be invested in stocks. The most popular is a mutual fund, because it is often the only choice in 401(k)s. Although there are a number of good mutual funds, most of them are not suitable for the retired investor. Funds have the advantage of allowing the investor to easily diversify, but they have more fees, less liquidity and often only a false promise of diversity. For example, a popular choice are target date mutual funds that become more conservative in their investment as you age. These are great while you are working and just accumulating money with little thought as to how best to invest it. They are not appropriate for you in retirement. Your first clue should be the target date of the fund, which is supposed to be the year you retire(d). If your fund is called something like Target2015, then it's time to wake up. 2015 is long gone and it ain't coming back.

ETFs are the easiest, most versatile, lowest fee and usually the most tax efficient. They are easiest because they can be traded just like any stock and unlike mutual funds, you never have to pay a broker any load fee, neither a front-end load when you buy it or a back-end load when you sell it. They are more versatile because of the huge, diverse and expanding population of special focus ETFs, as well as the fact that they can be traded anytime the market is open and you don't have to wait until the end of the day to buy or sell.

ETFs have the lowest fees. Just go to any financial website, such as Yahoo.com and compare the expense ratio of an ETF with a mutual fund. Even worse, mutual funds are allowed to collect hidden fees that are not counted in the expense ratio listed on financial sites. These are called 12b-1 fees and they basically allow mutual funds to charge you for the advertising that they have used to get you to buy their product. If this wasn't bad enough, the regulation is never investigated and rarely enforced so that companies can give parties for all their friends, call it market research and have you pay for it.

Finally, ETFs are more tax efficient. Managing your investments for tax efficiency is especially important for the retired investor. Upon retirement, we usually have more money sitting in taxable and non-taxable accounts than ever before. And we depend on that money lasting for the rest of our life. It won't last if we let the government collect high taxes every quarter. In addition, unmanaged taxable income can reduce your social security. ETFs will let you manage your taxes better than mutual funds. Mutual funds must distribute capital gains to the shareholder when a stock in the fund is sold for a profit. So a mutual fund holder will have capital gains whenever the mutual fund decides to sell something, which happens frequently. However, you only pay capital gains on an ETF when you sell the ETF. Therefore, you get to choose when you take capital gains and can do it when it is most tax efficient for you.

How to Buy an ETF

Buying an ETF is just like buying a stock. Buying and selling stocks and ETFs has gone through tremendous changes in the last decade, many of which are to the advantage of the retired investor. Previously, trading fees could easily eat up the unwary investor's capital, since it was not unusual to pay $100 or more for each trade. Today the individual investor can make trades for free.

The first thing is to make sure that you have a brokerage account--which is free to set up--and then fund it with the money you intend to invest. Once the account is ready, you can initiate a trade.

When you trade in a brokerage account, you will be offered choices about how the trade should be placed. The most common trade is a *limit order*. The investor puts in a maximum price that he is willing to pay for the ETF and the ETF is not bought unless it gets down to that price or below. This means that the trade may not happen if the price does not go down to or below your limit price. The buyer can also allow the limit order to expire at the end of the day or to continue until it is canceled or a number of days (usually 60) has passed. The investor needs to be careful when using Good Till Canceled since they are easy to forget and may make a trade when market conditions have changed so that you no longer wish to buy that ETF.

The buyer also has the choice of a market order which means that the ETF will be bought at the next available price. This is rarely a good idea, especially when the ETF or stock is thinly traded. Opportunistic traders can take advantage of a market order to sell you an ETF at a premium.

High Dividend ETFs

Most of your investments in Late Trending Up should be in a high dividend ETF.

A dividend is a portion of the company's profit that is paid to the shareholders. Over half of U.S. publicly traded companies pay some kind of dividend. It is usually only a fraction, but it can sometimes be more than the company's entire profit because the company is trying to maintain an established track record of paying dividends. Dividends are usually paid in cash, although they can be in shares in the company. The company can choose their own time frame for paying dividends, but they are usually paid quarterly, although it is not unusual to see special one-time dividends paid near the end of the year, usually for tax reasons.

High-yield means that the dividends are greater than the average dividend of the S&P 500, which is currently about 1.85%. A high yield often reflects a company's mature status. Since the business has relatively few profitable growth investments it can pursue, it returns most of its cash flow to shareholders in the form of dividends. Utilities, real estate, telecom, energy, financial, materials and health companies tend to pay dividends. Companies that are still growing and developing, such as technology or pharmaceutical companies, usually don't pay dividends since they feel that the best use of their profit is to re-invest in the company's growth. Because dividend companies are generally stable and mature, they tend to be less volatile than non-dividend stocks, and tend to decline less in recessions and crashes.

Some retired investors like to use dividends as a cash flow to live on. That way, they never have to touch their capital. This is a good idea if you want to make your undeserving brats fabulously wealthy when you die. Otherwise, treat your dividends just like any other cash, to be re-invested, kept in cash or spent according to your overall investment plan. The amount of dividends you get should have nothing to do with how much you withdraw.

Dividends are more tax efficient than ordinary income from a job, income from a pension, or withdrawing from a traditional IRA. Most dividends are "qualified," which means that they are taxed at a lower rate and are currently tax free for those in the less than 15% tax bracket. However, they are not as tax efficient as capital gains, because you have no control over when you receive them. Therefore you must keep an eye on the amount of dividends that you are receiving to make sure that they don't disrupt you tax planning.

There are a number of ETFs that focus on high-dividend stocks such as Vanguard High Dividend Yield (VYM), Fidelity High Dividend (FDVV) and ProShares S&P 500 Dividend Aristocrats (NOBL).

50% of the money that you have invested in Late Trending Up should be in a High Dividend ETF.

Diversifying for Profits

There are two kinds of diversification. What people usually mean by diversification is defensive diversification. That means diversifying in case your assumptions about the economy are wrong. For example, you may think that the market is and will continue to be Late Trending Up, but some glitch may happen and it may suddenly be in a Downturn. The superior investor always assumes that they may be wrong and prepares for that possibility by not investing all of their money in the current assumption.

A second kind of diversification is diversifying for profit. Here you choose a mix of the type of investments that will do well in the type of economy that you are assuming--in this case, Late Trending Up. This protects you from an unpredicted failure in one area and should give you as much profit with less risk. Therefore, although High-dividend ETFs should be your best investment in this market, we will diversify into other investments that promise to do almost as well.

Sector Momentum Trends

Companies are grouped into sectors with other similar companies. For example, Marathon Oil, Halliburton and Conoco Phillips are all in the Energy sector. This can be further divided into Industries. Marathon Oil and Conoco Phillips are both in the Oil, Gas & Consumable Fuels industry, while Haliburton is in the Energy Equipment & Services Industry. Stocks in the same Industry usually move up or down together. Sectors also move up and down together although they are more diverse.

There are ETFs that target a particular sector. I will list them with their Fidelity ETFs, although there are other investment companies with sector ETFs. There are eleven sectors: Communication Services (FCOM), Consumer Discretionary (FDIS), Consumer Staples (FSTA), Energy (FENY), Financials (FNCL), Health Care (FHLC), Industrials (FIDU), Information Technology (FTEC), Materials (FMAT), Real Estate (FREL) and Utilities (UTIL).

In a Late Trending Up economy, the Energy and Materials sectors usually do well, since businesses are still expanding and Energy and Materials aren't hurt by rising inflation. As Late Trending Up continues, investor will begin to see signs of increasing interest rates and a slowing economy. Then defensive sectors that do well in an economic slowdown grow stronger. These are Health Care, Consumer Staples and Utilities.

Create a chart in a charting website. I like PerfChart on StockCharts.com (they try to get you to buy access, but look around the website for the free charts) because it incorporates both the stock's price and its dividends to give a total return. Most other charting websites only show the price. Put in the ETFs for Energy, Materials, Consumer Staples, Health Care and Utilities so that you can see the trend lines since the start of the Late Trending Up period. We are going to compare their Momentum Trends.

Momentum is the tendency of an investment to persist in its trend. If it's going up, it tends to continue to go up, and if it's going down, it goes lower. A momentum strategy tries to take advantage of this tendency in the market. The strategy does not depend on looking at fundamentals or developing your own prediction of what the market will do. You cannot anticipate a trend; you can only identify one. You won't catch the first move higher; you will only jump on board after the train has left the station.

Momentum is sometimes referred to as a factor. There have been a number of factors identified that are supposed to identify market "anomalies" so that the investor can take advantage of them. Some of the better-known factors are small size, high quality, low volatility and hundreds of others that are less known. Studies have shown that the market underprices the stocks with the factors and suggests that those in the know can take advantage of this.

Unfortunately, these factors tend to disappear once the anomaly is known. For example, after a study has shown that the market underprices low-volatility stocks, investors are willing to pay more for them. The only factor that hasn't disappeared after the anomaly is revealed is momentum. In fact, momentum appears to have increased. If you think about it for a minute, you'll understand why. If people start paying a higher price for low-volatility stocks, then the anomaly disappears and future earnings will be right in line with the price paid. However, if people start to pay higher prices for stocks with momentum, the momentum will increase and push the price even higher, increasing the momentum. Of course, eventually the price will come back to reality, but meantime the anomaly increases and a momentum strategy pays off handsomely.

Examine the chart you've created that shows the trend of your sectors since the start of the Late Trending Up period. You want to invest about **10%** in whichever is doing best of Energy or Materials. And you should invest about **10%** in whatever sector is doing best of Consumer Staples, Health Care and Utilities. It should add up to a total of 20% of the money that's invested in Late Trending Up. Check your sectors every week while Late Trending Up continues and make adjustments to suit the trends, looking not at the immediate past, but at the trend since the start of the Late Trending Up market.

Small-cap ETF

Companies that pay high dividends are almost always large or mid-size corporations with very few small corporations. It is good to balance your investments with small corporations. The smaller companies do well when inflation is rising as it tends to do in the Late Trending Up market. Small companies are usually better able to pass on price increases to their customers, especially when the industry has a small customer base with few competitors.

10% of the money that you have invested in Late Trending Up should be in a Small-cap ETF, such as Vanguard's Small-Cap ETF (VB), iShares Russell 2000 Growth ETF (IWO) or Vanguard's Tax-Managed Small Cap Mutual Fund (VTMSX).

Developed Market International Equity ETF

The S&P 500 only invests in companies that are domiciled in the U.S. However, when U.S. stocks are doing well, the entire world is usually doing well also, and some countries are doing considerably better. Therefore, it is a good idea to have some investments outside the U.S. However, it should be noted that the S&P 500 is already international. Even though the companies are based in the U.S. 30% of the revenue of the S&P 500 companies come from outside the U.S.

The U.S. dollar is usually strong at this point in the cycle. Therefore, you can buy foreign stocks with U.S. dollars at a bargain. Currency exchange rates may fluctuate; the dollar may go down or foreign currency go up, but this is not wholly bad since it does provide some additional diversification. But the most important source of diversification is that the economic forces that are driving foreign markets are somewhat different from those driving U.S. markets.

There is always a home bias in stock investments. Japanese know more about Japanese stocks, Australians know more about Australian stock and Americans know more about U.S. stocks. So people tend to buy what they hear most about. The home bias is especially strong in a Late Rising Market, so foreign stocks are often underpriced.

The best investments will be in developed markets instead of emerging markets, since the latter are more susceptible to a downturn.

To increase the international exposure, the retired investor should have about 10% of the money invested for Late Trending Up in an international developed market ETF, such as iShares Core EAFE (IEFA) or Vanguard's FTSE Developed Markets ETF (VEA).

Transitioning to Cash

If you are in Late Trending Up, then you know that inflation will start to take off and the Federal Reserve will begin to raise interest rates. This means that, for the retired investor, this market is one of transition.

You are going to take some of your investments off the table while you are still ahead. This requires discipline, since the average investor tends to base their decisions on the past rather than future risk. When stocks are going up, the past looks marvelous even as future risks are increasing.

The Late Trending Up Market often begins setting records for the year (and this includes all-time records). Whenever the market sets a record for the year and it hasn't already set one in the last week, you should sell one percent of your investments and put them into cash. We are going to sell whatever stocks are doing best by rebalancing our investments. Originally, the amount of money that you have invested in 1) Foreign ETF, 2) Consumer Staples, Health Care or Utilities ETF, and 3) Energy or Materials ETF should be about the same. You should sell whatever you have more invested in until all the amounts invested are equal to the lowest one.

If the amount you sell is not equal to the one percent that we are trying to put into cash, look at your High Dividend ETF. It should be five times as high as the ten percent ETFs you just rebalanced. If it is higher, then sell as much of your High Dividend ETF as needed to reach one percent cash. If it is lower, then sell an equal amount from the Foreign ETF, Consumer Staples, Health Care or Utilities ETF, and Energy or Materials ETF to make the one percent.

In addition, every 6 months you should rebalance your portfolio into 50/10/10/10/10 balance by selling investments and putting them into cash. During Late Trending Up, rebalance only by selling, never by buying.

Once you have 30% of your investments in cash, quit transitioning to cash.

Transitioning to Bonds

As the Late Trending Up market continues, inflation will begin to rise and the Federal Reserve will begin to raise rates. The best time to buy bonds is when the Feds are through raising interest rates. As the Late Trending Up Market gets older, keep a close watch on interest rates. When your research indicates that they are near their highest, put all of your cash into Treasury bonds.

You can buy U.S. Treasury bonds directly online at TreasureyDirect.gov. But it is generally easier to buy them as part of an ETF. ETFs are term diversified and usually more liquid, being tradable anytime the stock market is open.

When you buy a bond, you are lending money to the bond seller. The seller might be a corporation, a city, the U.S or a foreign government. Most bonds incur three risks: 1) the borrower declares bankruptcy and you don't get paid back; 2) the borrower pays you off early and so you don't receive all the expected income; and 3) you want to sell the bond early and you can't get what you paid for it. None of these risks are believed to apply to U.S. treasuries.

However, there is a fourth risk that applies to every loan. It is inflation. This means that you'll get the money that you loaned back, but that amount of money won't be worth as much. When looking at the yield of a bond, you should also figure in inflation. Yield without inflation is called a nominal return. Yield with inflation is a *real* return. Looking at inflation, we see yet another way for bonds to diversify your holdings. Less-than-expected inflation generally hurts equities, but it is good for bonds.

Of course, there are many kinds of bonds, but Treasuries are the most defensive since they will move opposite of everything else that you'll invest in. If the market crashes, you will be able to sell your bonds at a profit and then invest them at the bottom and so regain the lion's share of your wealth during the fast upsurge that follows a crash.

Corporate Bonds will pay higher yield than treasuries, but they will provide little protection since they tend to go down when the market goes down. This is especially true of the higher yielding corporate bonds, often called junk bonds.

It is best to buy a long-term Treasury ETF, since those will give you the most protection. Vanguard's Long-Term Treasury Index Fund ETF (VGLT), SPDR Long Term Treasury ETF (SPTL) and Schwab Long-term US Treasury ETF (SCHQ) all have very low expense ratios.

In a **Late Trending Up** market, your beginning investments should look like below. As the market progresses, you will move more into cash and finally into bonds.

- **10%** in a **Cash**
- **50%** in a **High Dividend ETF**
- **10%** in **Energy or Materials Sector ETF**s
- **10%** in **Consumer Staples, Health Care or Utilities Sector ETF**s
- **10%** in a **Small-Cap ETF**
- **10%** in a **Developed Foreign Equity ETF**

11: Volatile Market

You are in the right chapter if the market has had frequent big price swings more or less within a range and it has been moving sideways, neither trending up or down.

Stocks are always more volatile than rational responses to actual events would dictate. These volatile markets tend to happen in the middle of an economic cycle, between Early Trending Up and Late Trending Up, or toward the end of Late Trending Up. Usually, monetary policy is neutral and most of the market movements are due to overreactions to somewhat good and somewhat bad news, or perhaps to a shifting political situation.

One overreaction leads to a counter overreaction, and so up-and-down movements tend to cluster. Similarly, one month of volatility means that the next month tends to be volatile. In such markets, we know that there will be large moves, but the direction of any particular move is essentially unpredictable.

At such a time, it is important to remember the difference between volatility and risk. Volatility is when the market is undergoing rapid and extreme price swings. Risk means that something bad, like losing your investment, might happen. Volatility, in-and-of-itself, is not risk. In fact, we can make money out of volatility by selling when the market is at one of its highs and buying when it is at one of its lows.

Traders often welcome volatility because it fits more with their short-term vision. Making quick profits is the name of their game and this is the market where that works best. Even if you just bought that stock a week ago, you sell it as it bounces back up, and then maybe buy it back the next week. However, there is a great danger with this profitable strategy. Sometimes, the market doesn't bounce back from its low, but keeps going down instead. Then you have bought stock just before a downturn, the worst time to buy.

Transition to the new market

Look at the percentages at the end of this section. Take the next six weeks to sell anything you own if it isn't on this list. If you have Momentum Stocks, sell them. Research has shown that the most efficient way to cash these in is to sell one-fifth of your overinvestments every week. You can skip one week of your choice, and you can double up one week, but it needs to be all sold in 6 weeks. Leave that money in cash while you are doing the selling.

Take another look at your macro forces to make sure you are in the right market, and then begin buying your new investments. Buy one-fifth of your new investments every week. You can skip one week of your choice, and you can double up one week, but it needs to be all bought in six weeks.

Determining How Much and Where to Diversify

The goal of investing is to grow your wealth and provide you with income for the rest of your life. However, with growth comes risk and the goal of diversification is to dampen that risk. Risk may be your friend when you're young and have income from working to get you through, but it can be devastating in retirement.

The greatest risks in a Volatile Market is that the Market doesn't come back up from one of its swings down, but instead becomes a downturn. The best protection in such cases, are U.S. Treasury bonds. Whatever your criticism of the U.S. government and its debt, buyers of bonds know that the U.S. is the safest guarantor in the world. Neither cash, nor gold, not bitcoins come close to matching the diversifying power of bonds backed by the full faith of the U.S. government.

Bonds

U.S. bonds usually have one of the lowest yields of any investment, but the importance of bonds is not their yield, but their safety. When equities and other growth investments are plunging, Treasury bonds are rising. When everyone is fleeing to safety, the safety they flee to are U.S. bonds.

You can buy U.S. Treasury bonds directly online at TreasureyDirect.gov. But it is generally easier to buy them as part of an ETF. ETFs are term diversified and usually more liquid, being tradable anytime the stock market is open.

When you buy a bond, you are lending money to the bond seller. The seller might be a corporation, a city, the U.S or a foreign government. Most bonds incur three risks: 1) the borrower declares bankruptcy and you don't get paid back; 2) the borrower pays you off early and so you don't receive all the expected income; and 3) you want to sell the bond early and you can't get what you paid for it. None of these risks are believed to apply to U.S. treasuries.

However, there is a fourth risk that applies to every loan. It is inflation. This means that you'll get the money that you loaned back, but that amount of money won't be worth as much. When looking at the yield of a bond, you should also figure in inflation. Yield without inflation is called a nominal return. Yield with inflation is a *real* return. Looking at inflation, we see yet another way for bonds to diversify your holdings. Less-than-expected inflation generally hurts equities, but it is good for bonds.

Of course, there are many kinds of bonds, but Treasuries are the most defensive. If the market crashes, you will be able to sell your bonds at a profit and then invest them at the bottom and so regain the lion's share of your wealth during the fast upsurge that follows a crash.

Corporate Bonds will pay higher yield than treasuries, but they will provide little protection since they tend to go down when the market goes down. This is especially true of the higher yielding corporate bonds, often called junk bonds. When Treasury yields are down, the average asshole investor will "chase returns" and buy junk bonds to get the higher return that he feels is necessary. This is never a good idea. Junk bonds are priced off of Treasuries. When Treasury yields are down, so are junk bond yields. That means that you are getting less reward for more risk. The successful investor is always looking for more reward for less risk.

It is best to buy a long-term Treasury ETF, since those will give you the most protection. Vanguard's Long-Term Treasury Index Fund ETF (VGLT), SPDR Long Term Treasury ETF (SPTL) and Schwab Long-term US Treasury ETF (SCHQ) all have very low expense ratios.

To Diversify, **10%** of your money in a Volatile Market should be in a long-term Treasury ETF.

Exchange Traded Funds (ETFs)

You should be invested in stocks during a Volatile Market. Although there are many ups and downs, historically stocks have made 5% to 7% in a Volatile Market.

There are several ways in which you can be invested in stocks. The most popular is a mutual fund, because it is often the only choice in 401(k)s. Although there are a number of good mutual funds, most of them are not suitable for the retired investor. Funds have the advantage of allowing the investor to easily diversify, but they have more fees, less liquidity and often only a false promise of diversity. For example, a popular choice are target date mutual funds that become more conservative in their investment as you age. These are great while you are working and just accumulating money with little thought as to how best to invest it. They are not appropriate for you in retirement. Your first clue should be the target date of the fund, which is supposed to be the year you retire(d). If your fund is called something like Target2015, then it's time to wake up. 2015 is long gone and it ain't coming back.

ETFs are the easiest, most versatile, lowest fee and usually the most tax efficient. They are easiest because they can be traded just like any stock and unlike mutual funds, you never have to pay a broker any load fee, neither a front-end load when you buy it or a back-end load when you sell it. They are more versatile because of the huge, diverse and expanding population of special focus ETFs, as well as the fact that they can be traded anytime the market is open and you don't have to wait until the end of the day to buy or sell.

ETFs have the lowest fees. Just go to any financial website, such as Yahoo.com and compare the expense ratio of an ETF with a mutual fund. Even worse, mutual funds are allowed to collect hidden fees that are not counted in the expense ratio listed on financial sites. These are called 12b-1 fees and they basically allow mutual funds to charge you for the advertising that they have used to get you to buy their product. If this wasn't bad enough, the regulation is never investigated and rarely enforced so that companies can give parties for all their friends, call it market research and have you pay for it.

Finally, ETFs are more tax efficient. Managing your investments for tax efficiency is especially important for the retired investor. Upon retirement, we usually have more money sitting in taxable and non-taxable accounts than ever before. And we depend on that money lasting for the rest of our life. It won't last if we let the government collect high taxes every quarter. In addition, unmanaged taxable income can reduce your social security. ETFs will let you manage your taxes better than mutual funds. Mutual funds must distribute capital gains to the shareholder when a stock in the fund is sold for a profit. So a mutual fund holder will have capital gains whenever the mutual fund decides to sell something, which happens frequently. However, you only pay capital gains on an ETF when you sell the ETF. Therefore, you get to choose when you take capital gains and can do it when it is most tax efficient for you.

How to Buy an ETF

Buying an ETF is just like buying a stock. Buying and selling stocks and ETFs has gone through tremendous changes in the last decade, many of which are to the advantage of the retired investor. Previously, trading fees could easily eat up the unwary investor's capital, since it was not unusual to pay $100 or more for each trade. Today the individual investor can make trades for free.

The first thing is to make sure that you have a brokerage account--which is free to set up--and then fund it with the money you intend to invest. Once the account is ready, you can initiate a trade.

When you trade in a brokerage account, you will be offered choices about how the trade should be placed. The most common trade is a *limit order*. The investor puts in a maximum price that he is willing to pay for the ETF and the ETF is not bought unless it gets down to that price or below. This means that the trade may not happen if the price does not go down to or below your limit price. The buyer can also allow the limit order to expire at the end of the day or to continue until it is canceled or a number of days (usually 60) has passed. The investor needs to be careful when using Good Till Canceled since they are easy to forget and may make a trade when market conditions have changed so that you no longer wish to buy that ETF.

The buyer also has the choice of a market order which means that the ETF will be bought at the next available price. This is rarely a good idea, especially when the ETF or stock is thinly traded. Opportunistic traders can take advantage of a market order to sell you an ETF at a premium.

Low Volatility ETFs

Most of your investments in a Volatile Market should be in low-volatility ETFs. In all markets except Early Trending Up, low-volatility stocks do as well or better than the market, but they do especially well in a Volatile Market as investor become nervous and fearful about the market's gyrations and flee to low volatility.

Many investors have been told by the pundits and MBA imbeciles that more volatility means greater returns. The average asshole therefore prefers stocks with the potential for spectacular jumps in price so that they can dream of all the money they'll have when their ship finally comes in. However, when we look at the return-to-risk ratio, low-volatility stocks do substantially better, especially in high volatility market.

High-volatility stocks, like biotech companies, can make their owners rich if their research and development pays off. But they are even more likely to lose money, when a line of expensive and time-consuming R&D doesn't pay off. Low-volatility stocks are usually established companies with stable earnings, a proven business model and a boring, but steady increase in their value.

Low-volatility stocks typically have the following characteristics: steady earnings, above-average margins, efficient use of assets, and low debt. They also have what Warren Buffet calls a "wide moat." This means that the company has a sustainable advantage over its competitors. That advantage might be simply a recognizable brand name, such as Apple or Pepsi, or the warehouses, supply chains and built-in efficiencies that would cost any competitor a great deal to replicate, such as Amazon or Walmart.

Low-volatility stocks tend to occur in some industries more than others, so the investor should be aware that they may be unintentionally overweighting some sectors. For example, consumer staples, utilities and real estate tend to have low volatility while tech stocks, small caps, and energy tend to have high volatility. A number of investment sites, such as finance.yahoo.com under Holdings, will show you the sectors that an ETF currently is invested in. Keep the overweighting in mind when you are choosing your other investments.

40% of the money that you have invested for a Volatile Market should be in a U.S. low-volatility equities ETF, such as Invesco S&P 500 Low Volatility ETF (SPLV) or the iShares Edge MSCI Minimum Volatility USA ETF (USMV).

For further diversity, **30%** of the money that you have invested for a Volatile Market should be in a Global low-volatility equities ETF, such as iShares Edge MSCI Min Vol EAFE ETF (EFAV) or Vanguard Global Minimum Volatility Fund (VMVSX).

Active funds

In a number of important ways, the interests of the fund manager diverge from the client's interests. Because all fund managers today have gone through a form of Pavlovian training called business school and have therefore been taught that people are supposed to be greedy and think only of their own interests, there are only a few fund managers that can be trusted. And I'm afraid that most of them will retire soon or die. Nevertheless, during a Volatile Market, it is worth the time to find a fund manager who has some semblance of integrity. A good fund manager with access to cheap money, willing to dig into the data and with a track record of superior investing could be invaluable.

What you want in a Volatile Market is somebody with a lot of freedom to look anywhere for those deals that will constantly emerge when the financial tide goes out. And to be able to get out when the financial waves dash them against the shore.

10% of what you invest for a Volatile Market should be in an actively managed fund such as Wasatch Global Opportunities Fund (WAGOX) where the superior investor, J.B. Taylor has been since 2011, or Seven Canyons World Innovators Fund (WAGTX) where Joshua Stewart, also superior, has been since 2012.

Value Stocks

Value stocks are a term that many people have tried to give a precise, mathematical definition--for example, the 30% of stocks with the highest book-to-market values. It is because of such misleading definitions that you will hear that value investing is dead. A better definition of value stocks are those stocks where the current valuation is lower than it should be for its past and projected earnings. In other words, stocks that are cheap for the amount of money they produce. For value investing, the important thing is not what you buy, but what you pay for it.

Those who believe in the efficient market theory, don't think that there are any value stocks. They believe that the market price perfectly reflects the stock's value. There's a story about an economic professor and a superior investor walking down the street together when they come across a $100 bill laying on the sidewalk. The economic professor says, "It can't really be a $100 bill, otherwise somebody would have picked it up." The professor walks away and the superior investor picks up the bill and treats himself to a wonderful dinner. The moral is: don't leave profits lying there just because others don't believe in their value.

Rather than the efficient market, Benjamin Graham, the guru of value investing, says the superior investor should think of themselves as partner in a business with a manic-depressive named Mr. Market. Every day Mr. Market offers to buy out the investor's stake or sell his own. Some days he offers a reasonable price, sometimes it's too high or too low. The job of the value investor is to have a good enough sense of what the business is worth to know when to cut a deal with Mr. Market and when to ignore him.

Value investing depends upon being able to outthink the market consensus. You are not just looking for a good company; you are looking for a good company that others think is not-so-good so that the price is low. That means that you have to know which is a good company and how your view compares with what other people are willing to pay. In the best case, you will know why other investors price the stock lower and why they are wrong. You have to know both investing and investor psychology. That gives you two chances to be wrong.

It is easier to find values if you start with what is unpopular, especially if you look at the sources of unwarranted unpopularity. Unpopularity is the value investor's friend. Fortunately, today there are some sources of unwarranted unpopularity that are easy for the value investor to exploit. It has to do with the way that sector ETFs work.

Sector ETFs have been a boon to both professional and individual investors. They let investors move quickly into a diversified position in a particular sector. Sectors are groupings of companies with other similar companies. For example, Marathon Oil, Halliburton and Conoco Phillips are all in the Energy sector. This can be further divided into Industries. Marathon Oil and Conoco Phillips are both in the Oil, Gas & Consumable Fuels industry, while Haliburton is in the Energy Equipment & Services Industry. Stocks in the same Industry usually move up or down together. Sectors also move up and down together although they are more diverse. It is that diversity that the value investor can exploit.

The trading volume of sector ETFs is so large today that they move the market. Since sector ETFs buy and sell all the companies in the sector, a popular sector will raise the price of all the companies whether they deserve it or not. And, more to the point, an unpopular sector will lower the price of all the companies, even those that can be expected to do well. The value investor will look for companies that are doing well even though their sector's price is down. Those are the companies that the value investor wants to buy, good companies in an unpopular sector.

The first step is to identify what sectors are underpriced. There are a number of places to go for analysis of sectors (both Fidelity and Charles Schwab have sector analyses that are on the web and available to the public). However, the easiest to use is Morningstar's Fair Value at https://www.morningstar.com/market-fair-value. They have charts that will show you which sectors are undervalued or overvalued. Use the pull-down menu on the left to go through each of the sectors to find which are undervalued. Once you've identified one or two undervalued sectors, you will try to identify which companies are undeservedly undervalued.

To identify good companies in an undervalued sector, go to a Stock Screener that allows you to screen for Sector, PEG (Price/Earnings-to-Growth) and size. Fidelity has an easy to use Stock Screener at https://research2.fidelity.com/pi/stock-screener#strategies. On the left side, under Basic Company Facts, you will find Sector/Industry/Sub-industry. Choose the sector that you've identified as undervalued. While you are there at Basic Company Facts go under Security Type and choose Common Stock. Then go to Market Capitalization and choose Large Cap, Medium Cap and Small cap. You aren't going to look at Mega and micro caps, because Mega caps establish the consensus view and therefore aren't going to go against the consensus and Micro caps are too idiosyncratic. Next go under Company Value and choose the PEG Ratio. You are looking for a PEG ratio that is between one and zero. The lower the PEG ratio, the more undervalued the stock is, except that negative values indicate that there were negative earnings. The Stock Screener should have produced a list of your most likely investments.

Take that list of stocks produced by the Stock Screener to another site that gives values for companies. I like CNN Business's Forecast page, https://www.cnn.com/business/. Put your stock's ticker symbol into their Quote Search field and look under Forecast. You can also go to TD Ameritrade, https://invest.ameritrade.com/, put in your ticker symbol and look under valuation. (Making a small investment through their site will give you access to all of their research tools.) You are looking for stocks that are undervalued and yet different enough from the overall sector to be less affected by whatever the consensus thinks is diminishing the value of the sector.

You have a list of stocks, but don't buy them yet. Keep your investments in Cash until the next time your Volatile Market goes down. Then, you'll have some stocks to buy that should go up even higher when the market goes back up and yet not go down as much should the market fall further. That's the value of value stocks: there is more upside when the market goes up and less downside when it goes down.

Cash

When investors say cash, they don't just mean actual dollar bills. Cash includes money-market funds, cash-management accounts maintained by brokers and short-term Treasuries. The important features are that these have very low volatility and are liquid, i.e. you can get your money out within a day or less.

The most convenient place for the investor to keep cash is in a broker's cash-managed account. These are usually swept every night into FDIC insured bank accounts and they often pay competitive interest rates. However, you must check to be sure that this is true, since some brokers depend on convenience alone to attract your money.

Money market funds and money market accounts are tied to short-term fixed income investments like U.S. Treasuries. They usually pay a bit more than savings accounts and broker cash-managed accounts. Money market *funds* are not FDIC insured against losses, but money market *accounts* are.

Short-term treasuries usually pay a little more than money-markets but they are a bit more volatile and not quite as liquid because you must wait for a buyer before you can access the money. Normally that is not a problem, but it could become a problem during times of extreme stress when you most need to pull the money out.

For Diversification and transitioning into cash, you should put your money into your broker's cash-management funds that pay competitive interest rates and are insured, such as Vanguard Federal Money Market or Fidelity

Money Market Fund. If your broker doesn't automatically put your uninvested cash into a Money Market account. Find out how that can be arranged.

You will start off with 10% of your money in Cash. As you identify Value Stock, you will buy them with that cash until you have 10% of your money invested in Value Stocks.

10% of the money invested in a Volatile Market will be in either Cash or Value Stocks.

Rebalancing

As time passes, the vagaries of the market will change your investment allocations. If Treasuries do really well, they may soon make up more than 10% of your investments. Rebalancing means selling and buying investments to bring you back to your original allocations. This means that you are buying those investments that performed the worst and selling those that performed the best. This may feel anti-intuitive, but research has proven this to be the best strategy. It sounds better if you say that you are buying low and selling high.

In a **Volatile** market, your investments should look like this:

- **10%** in a **Long-term Treasury ETF**
- **40%** in a **Low-volatility U.S. ETF**
- **30%** in a **Low-volatility Global ETF**
- **10%** in an **Active Fund**
- **0-10%** in a **Value Stocks**
- **10-0%** in **Cash**

12: Downturn

If you've turned to this chapter, you must have the feeling that a recession could be on its way. I can tell you that you're right. You can count on it. A recession is coming. The only question is when.

A recession is a normal part of the business cycle. It is usually preceded by a downturn in the stock market. You could say that a downturn in the stock market is a predictor of a recession except that there are many downturns in the stock market that are followed by an uptick in economic activity. Indeed, people get so tired of hearing "wolf" shouted at every stock market downturn that they're not prepared when the real recession finally appears. In general, we only know that we are in a recession after we are already well entrenched. The superior investor prepares for an eventual recession instead of trying to predict precisely when it will happen.

In the modern economy, recessions typically appear when there is a widespread and prolonged decline in spending usually triggered by some event such as a mortgage crisis, the bursting of a speculative bubble, a shock to the trading system, a change in interest rates or a price surge in a necessary commodity. Or sometimes, shit just happens.

Recessions have two main effects on the ordinary person: unemployment and a significant loss of savings. You might think that the first one doesn't affect the retired person, but it does. People who are without a job or who fear they may be without a job cut back even more on their spending creating a vicious cycle where the recession gets deeper and deeper. That means that the stocks that the retired person has invested their savings in go down ever lower.

The worse the recession, the more people reduce their spending. The more people reduce spending, the worse the recession. This adverse feedback loop is the hallmark of a recession. Everyone is pursuing their own rational self-interest. Consumers are pulling back on purchases. Businesses are cutting investments and laying off workers. Banks are restricting lending. Investors are pulling out their money as fast as possible, willing to take whatever loss is necessary to get their hands on some cash. And this all adds up to a worse and worse recession. In fact, a recession can be triggered just by people thinking there will be a recession.

Most recessions start off looking like a stock market correction. In fact, it is impossible to tell whether the downturn will turn into the widespread and prolonged economic decline of a recession or will just be an adjustment of the stock market to more realistic values. If it's a correction, the downturn will last less than two months and the investor should use the opportunity to buy stocks at bargain prices. If it's going to turn into a recession, buying stocks is the last thing that the investor should do. The superior investor must accept that there is no sure-fire way to tell the difference. As with so much in investing, you must have a strategy that takes into account the risk that either could happen.

For the young investor, the strategy is simple: stay in as the market goes down and try to buy more while prices are cheap. If you have 30 or 40 years to recover, a recession is just a buying opportunity. However, once you're retired, you have two things working against you. One, you are taking money out to live on and if you're doing this during a recession, that means that you are selling low and baking in your losses. Two, you don't have the decades that may be necessary to recover. As one retired friend quipped, "A recession is worse than a divorce. You lose half your money and you still have a wife."

Since the end of World War II, a recession has hit the U.S. on an average of every six years. Even though it is impossible to predict when a recession will happen, they do show some common precursors. It is common for the market to have substantially appreciated in the previous two years and this is often at the end of a strong decade. There is some type of triggering event, usually a complex new financial instrument--such as investment trusts, derivatives or securitized mortgages--fails to perform as thought. The government will introduce political uncertainty into an already unstable situation and then will wait until the worst time to intervene in a way that makes the problem worse, such as restricting international trade or strengthening the dollar.

Of course, if all of these happen, it still doesn't mean that there will be a recession, but it does mean that it is likely. Whether lightning will strike this time, we don't know, but it is wise to seek some shelter when you see the thunderclouds rolling in.

Recessions usually don't last that long. The average duration of post-WWII recessions is 11 months and the stock market usually recovers even before the economy. However, recessions can take decades to recover from. Japan had a recession in the 90's that it still has not fully recovered from and it took over five years for the U.S. stock market to recover from the 2008 recession.

There is every reason to believe that the next recession will be a long and deep one. Most of the tools that help us recover from a recession are already stretched near their max. Deficient spending is setting records and interest rates are already near all-time lows. Even new, experimental programs for recovery, such as Quantitative Easing, are still in place from the last recession, even though nobody knows what their long-term side-effects will be. And it is hard to believe that we can muster the political consensus to save central institutions as we did in the last recession for automobiles and banks. In fact, it is increasingly difficult to see the government able to do anything that could halt the adverse feedback loop that creates a long and deep recession. Nevertheless, this does not mean that the next downturn will turn into a long and deep recession. Before the next recession, we could have a dozen corrections or just a long, slow economic stagnation. But the retired investor must always keep in mind the possibility of a recession. For the retired investor, avoiding or mitigating the devastating effects of a recession are much more important than any missed investment opportunities in a correction.

You've already done four things right to prepare for a possible recession.

1. You've set aside cash for one year of necessary and discretionary expenses and another year of necessary expenses.
2. You've diversified your investments so that if a recession hits, some part of your investments will do well.
3. You've avoided Fear of Missing Out, so that you kept back some extra cash when everyone else was fully invested in the melt-up before the crash.
4. You've prepared options for a long recession, for example, you are ready for a second career if necessary.

Now you must watch the market and look for the signals that it's time to protect your savings and to set aside some cash to invest when the economy recovers. You will do this knowing full well that you will miss a buying opportunity, but for the retired investor, the risk of losing your money in a recession is more critical than the risk of missing a buying opportunity.

Given this, the retired investor should have two primary goals for a downturn: 1) protect their savings; and 2) have some cash to invest when the economy recovers. To accomplish this, the retired investor must ignore two of the most repeated commandments of the investing pundits. Despite all of the advice you've heard, you **should not** Buy and Hold and you *should* try to Time the Market.

The advice to Buy and Hold and to not Time the Market are meant for the average investor who is saving for their eventual retirement. He doesn't have the time to study the market and he has plenty of time to recover. However, the retired investor has plenty of time to study the market and doesn't have the time to recover. Buy and Hold would only make sense for the retired investor if you aren't going to need to withdraw any money for the next 20 years. But if that's you, you don't really need to invest at all and therefore it is unlikely that you'd be reading this book.

At every downturn, you will see a parade of pundits calmly advising everyone to "stay the course." Of course, it's never a good idea to panic sell, but that doesn't mean that your personal savings should stay on board and go down with the ship. The retired investor cannot afford to "stay the course." You have to have a strategy set up to protect your savings.

Seven & Eleven Percent

"The Dow plunges to its Lowest Point since Yesterday"

"Millions of Dollars Lost in Market! Investors Search Behind Sofa Cushions"

"Record Number of Stocks Dive Below their Record Highs"

Don't pay attention to any headlines like these. You are going to look at one thing: the S&P's percentage decline since the last high. Go to your favorite charting web site and set your view so that you can see the percent change from the last high. I use the charts on finance.yahoo.com. Have it chart SPY (an index fund for the S&P 500) for the last six months. Note the date of the highest point and go into *Date Range* and have the chart start at that point and if you leave the stopping point blank it will end with today's quote. To get it to show the chart in percentage, go into *Comparison* and have it compare to S&P 500. On the right of the chart, you should be able to see the percentage change.

When the S&P 500 goes down **7%** from the last high, you are going to start to move 10% of your investments to cash. These numbers have been derived from repeated Monte Carlo simulations. Every prediction carries some risk, but these numbers are chosen to provide the best return over the spectrum of possible market moves. The quants in my office spent a number of years testing and perfecting this model. I asked them to explain it to me once.

"Do you understand quantum mechanics?" they asked.

"No."

"Then this is something else you won't understand."

To choose what to sell, create a new chart to see the movement of all your investments on one chart. On Yahoo finance charts, keep adding each investment through *Comparison* until you are able to compare the movements of all your investments. Sell those investments that are going down the fastest until you have sold 10% of your total investment. Leave that in cash until it is clear that the market has changed from Downturn into another kind of market, such as Volatile or Early Trending Up.

We sell these investments knowing full well that the stocks that have gone down the fastest may be those that will rise the fastest after we sell them. Because we know that we can't tell whether a downturn is a correction or a budding recession, we privilege safety over an investment opportunity. The market may jump back up as soon as we sell and those people who stayed in may make more money than we will, but we will be safer because that is more important for the retired investor.

In addition, you should stop withdrawing spending money from your investments. You have set aside one year of necessities in savings for just this predicament. Now is the time to live off the money that you have in cash equivalents instead of selling any more investments.

At 7% downturn you should
1. **Sell 10% of Investments**
2. **Take Living Expenses from Savings**

Continue to monitor the percentage decline of the stock market. If it goes back up, then identify the kind of market it is--Volatile, Early Trending Up, Late Trending Up--and change your investments to fit that market. There is no need to be in a hurry. Remember the psychological tendency, Fear Of Missing Out, and don't let that bias steer you.

If the market continues down, you must begin to implement your **11%** strategy. Again, the goal here is to protect your savings from a possible recession instead of taking advantage of possible investments. Let others make money betting that the market will come back up. They may be right, but we can't take that risk.

When the market goes down 11%, you must sell all the rest of your equities. When the market goes down 11%, historical trend analysis tells us that there is a greater than 50% probability that it will end up going down more than 20%. As the market plunges past an 11% downturn, many investors are forced to sell for various reasons, sometimes they just need the money now, but more often they have what is termed, a "margin call."

When investors buy equities with funds borrowed from the broker, that is called buying on margin. The stock that the investor buys is used as collateral on the loan. If the worth of the stock goes below a given percentage of the loan, the broker will issue a margin call which means that the investor must put up more money or the broker will sell the stock. Few investors want to put up more money when their stocks are plummeting, so they sell the stock at a loss. This, of course, sends the price of the stock even lower, which prompts even more selling. Those who sell at an 11% loss will miss all of that forced selling as the price dives ever lower.

It doesn't matter if you're selling things for a loss. Just sell all of your equities when the market is down 11%. Don't hang on until it comes back up. Whatever the market is going to do has nothing to do with whether you made or lost money on an investment. Now you are in a different market than you were in when you bought that losing investment. Yesterday's market may have told you to buy that investment, but Today's market has just plunged 11%. Today's market is telling you to sell all your equities.

Put half the money immediately into bonds and leave the rest in cash.

At 11% downturn you should
1. **Sell all Investments**
2. **Continue to take Living Expenses from Savings**

Bonds

You can buy U.S. Treasury bonds directly online at TreasureyDirect.gov. But it is generally easier to buy them as part of an ETF. ETFs are term diversified and usually more liquid, being tradable anytime the stock market is open.

Of course, there are many kinds of bonds, but Treasuries are the most defensive since they will move opposite to equities. If the market crashes, you will be able to sell your bonds at a profit and then invest them at the bottom and so regain the lion's share of your wealth during the fast upsurge that follows a crash.

Corporate Bonds will pay higher yield than treasuries, but they will provide little protection since they tend to go down when the market goes down. This is especially true of the higher yielding corporate bonds, often called junk bonds.

It is best to buy a long-term Treasury ETF, since those will give you the most protection. Vanguard's Long-Term Treasury Index Fund ETF (VGLT), SPDR Long Term Treasury ETF (SPTL) and Schwab Long-term US Treasury ETF (SCHQ) all have very low expense ratios.

However, bonds are only a temporary safe haven. Typically, they hit their high point one-to-two months after the event that triggered the recession. Look for a point to bank your profits from the bonds and move all your money into cash.

Cash

When investors say cash, they don't just mean actual dollar bills. Cash includes money-market funds, cash-management accounts maintained by brokers and short-term Treasuries. The important features are that these have very low volatility and are liquid, i.e. you can get your money out within a day or less.

The most convenient place for the investor to keep cash is in a broker's cash-managed account. These are usually swept every night into FDIC insured bank accounts and they often pay competitive interest rates. However, you must check to be sure that this is true, since some brokers depend on convenience alone to attract your money.

Money market funds and money market accounts are tied to short-term fixed income investments like U.S. Treasuries. They usually pay a bit more than savings accounts and broker cash-managed accounts. Money market *funds* are not FDIC insured against losses, but money market *accounts* are.

Short-term treasuries usually pay a little more than money-markets but they are a bit more volatile and not quite as liquid because you must wait for a buyer before you can access the money. Normally that is not a problem, but it could become a problem during times of extreme stress when you most need to pull the money out.

For transitioning into cash, you should put your money into your broker's cash-management funds that pay competitive interest rates and are insured, such as Vanguard Federal Money Market or Fidelity Money Market Fund. This allows you to buy when the market recovers and yet still gives you little volatility and an acceptable return while you wait. If your broker doesn't automatically put your uninvested cash into a Money Market account, find out how that can be arranged.

Buying Back In

The best time to buy equities is when the recession has hit bottom. Markets act like rubber bands, the farther they are stretched down, the more they snap back up. And yet this is when the average asshole gets out. Because they have no plan to deal with a recession, the average investor stay in the market as it plunges and then sell when the pain is the worst and they just can't stand it anymore. As the market makes its most reliable profits, the average investor sits safely on his cash and misses the best opportunities of a lifetime. The superior investor has prepared for this recession and is sitting on cash as the market hits its lowest point and starts to come back up. For the superior investor, a recession just means that the stocks he wants to buy are on sale.

Of course, the trick is to know when the market has hit bottom. Some people watch the VIX--a measure of the stock market's expectation of volatility as shown by S&P index options. Others watch the flow of investments into mutual funds. Some study the ascension of Mercury across Virgo. These are all about equally good. Make your best guess but don't trust it.

Normally, after a recession you would be in Early Trending Up, but it is certainly possible to be in an All-weather Market or even a Volatile. Look again at your macro trends, decide what Market you're in and go to that chapter.

Surviving a Long Recession

Of course, any recession has the potential to derail your retirement, but a long recession near the start of your retirement is the worst possible scenario. Given the current economic and political situation, you must be prepared for this. You cannot deal with a long recession with just an investment strategy. You must be prepared for lifestyle changes.

First of all, you must cut back on your spending. This is a good idea in any recession, but in a long recession, it could be a matter of survival. In a long recession, not only will you lose a chunk of your investments, but you can expect all social safety nets to shred. Public transportation, subsidized housing and even Medicare and social security could be drastically cut. Even if you limit your losses in the market, you may find yourself paying more for some necessities.

An inevitable recession is the reason that you divided your spending in the spreadsheet between necessary and discretionary spending. A long recession is the time to limit your discretionary spending. The good thing is that everyone else will be cutting back, so it will be easy for you to cut back on restaurants and entertain at people's homes instead.

The culture will also help you decrease discretionary spending. You'll see lots of stories about CEOs who ride subways, make their own coffee and have a side hustle. Morning programs will feature penny-pinching alternatives. The characters in sit-coms will be humorously frugal. Lifetime movies will feature the dramatically downward mobile who are still happy after all. All your friends will be cutting back to having one house, one car, staycations. And so, it will be easy for you to cut back too. In fact, having thought about it and planned for it ahead of time, you should be ahead of the curve and a leader of the trend.

You will find that some delayed gratification during a recession is pleasant. This is what study after study has shown. Delayed gratification allows you to enjoy the pleasures of planning and anticipation without the inevitable disappointments of reality. Research has shown that even something as trivial as a piece of chocolate will taste better to us when we delay and anticipate eating it. How much truer this is of those things that involve planning. When you think back, wasn't the planning of your vacation as much or even more fun than the vacation itself? Just putting off a vacation for a year, gives you a year more of the pleasure of planning and anticipating and keeps you from spending down your savings when you are most vulnerable.

This is also the time to put more effort into your second career. For those who have enjoyed their career, keeping a hand in during retirement is a pleasant thing. A recent survey showed that those over 65 who still work have some of the highest life satisfaction. Over 70% said that they were very satisfied with their work. If you are still doing some contract or part-time work in retirement, this may be a good time to ramp it up.

If you are one of those who hated their job and have instead developed a new skill, this is the time to put it into a higher gear. If you've already developed a craft and found some markets, it's a good time to put a little more effort into expanding your sales. If you've bought some rentals and hired a management company to take care of them, this is a good time to dispense with the management company and get more personally involved. If you're doing AirBnB, look for more days when you can open it up to guests.

If you haven't followed my previous advice to prepare a fun and lucrative second career, then this may be a good time to look for a part-time job. There are almost always low-paying, dead-end jobs in the service industry. You wouldn't want to take such a job if you were trying to build a career, but in retirement, a job in a coffee shop, bookstore or hardware store can be fun for a year or two. Pick a place that you wouldn't mind hanging out in anyway. It won't bring in a lot of money, but as we saw in chapter 4, even $10,000 a year can make a huge difference in your retirement outcome.

13: All-weather Market

You are in the right chapter if the market doesn't match any of the other four that we've identified.

When the market doesn't conform to any of the four types, we want to choose investments that do not correlate with each other, so that if economic growth slows, part of our investments will do well; if economic growth increases, part of our investments will do well; if inflation is higher than expected, part of our investments will do well; if inflation is lower than expected, part of our investments will do well. This is sometimes called an all-weather portfolio.

Fear of Missing Out

The greatest threat to an all-weather portfolio is FOMO or fear of missing out. An All-weather Market means that we don't know what will happen. We can protect ourselves from the bad things that may happen, but good times are just as likely to come. If the economy takes off and inflation stays low, we will not be in a position to reap all the rewards that others may be getting. That is part of our strategy. Retired investors must, above all, protect themselves from large losses. We must also make some money from our investments, but we are not going to swing for the fences. The average asshole might see the money that others are making in an unpredictable market and decide that he too must go all in. That is a mistake. The superior investor will stay disciplined and remember that missing out on some of the highs is part of the overall strategy.

Transition to the new market

Look at the percentages at the end of this section. Take the next six weeks to sell anything you own if it isn't on this list. If you have a bond fund, sell it. If you have Value Stocks, sell them. Research has shown that the most efficient way to cash these in is to sell one-fifth of your overinvestments every week. You can skip one week of your choice, and you can double up one week, but it needs to be all sold in 6 weeks. Leave that money in cash while you are doing the selling.

As money frees up, use it to buy your new investments. You can skip two weeks of your choice. Before each buy, take another look at your macro forces to make sure you are in the right market. You should have all your new investments bought in seven weeks.

Diversification
An All-weather Portfolio is already as Diversified as possible. It doesn't need further diversification.

Exchange Traded Funds (ETFs)
There are several ways in which you can be invested in stocks. The most popular is a mutual fund, because it is often the only choice in 401(k)s. Although there are a number of good mutual funds, most of them are not suitable for the retired investor. Funds have the advantage of allowing the investor to easily diversify, but they have more fees, less liquidity and often only a false promise of diversity. For example, a popular choice are target date mutual funds that become more conservative in their investment as you age. These are great while you are working and just accumulating money with little thought as to how best to invest it. They are not appropriate for you in retirement. Your first clue should be the target date of the fund, which is supposed to be the year you retire(d). If your fund is called something like Target2015, then it's time to wake up. 2015 is long gone and it ain't coming back.

ETFs are the easiest, most versatile, lowest fee and usually the most tax efficient. They are easiest because they can be traded just like any stock and unlike mutual funds, you never have to pay a broker any load fee, neither a front-end load when you buy it or a back-end load when you sell it. They are more versatile because of the huge, diverse and expanding population of special focus ETFs, as well as the fact that they can be traded anytime the market is open and you don't have to wait until the end of the day to buy or sell.

ETFs have the lowest fees. Just go to any financial website, such as Yahoo.com and compare the expense ratio of an ETF with a mutual fund. Even worse, mutual funds are allowed to collect hidden fees that are not counted in the expense ratio listed on financial sites. These are called 12b-1 fees and they basically allow mutual funds to charge you for the advertising that they have used to get you to buy their product. If this wasn't bad enough, the regulation is never investigated and rarely enforced so that companies can give parties for all their friends, call it market research and have you pay for it.

Finally, ETFs are more tax efficient. Managing your investments for tax efficiency is especially important for the retired investor. Upon retirement, we usually have more money sitting in taxable and non-taxable accounts than ever before. And we depend on that money lasting for the rest of our life. It won't last if we let the government collect high taxes every quarter. In addition, unmanaged taxable income can reduce your social security. ETFs will let you manage your taxes better than mutual funds. Mutual funds must distribute capital gains to the shareholder when a stock in the fund is sold for a profit. So a mutual fund holder will have capital gains whenever the mutual fund decides to sell something, which happens frequently. However, you only pay capital gains on an ETF when you sell the ETF. Therefore, you get to choose when you take capital gains and can do it when it is most tax efficient for you.

How to Buy an ETF
Buying an ETF is just like buying a stock. Buying and selling stocks and ETFs has gone through tremendous changes in the last decade, many of which are to the advantage of the retired investor. Previously, trading fees

could easily eat up the unwary investor's capital, since it was not unusual to pay $100 or more for each trade. Today the individual investor can make trades for free.

The first thing is to make sure that you have a brokerage account--which is free to set up--and then fund it with the money you intend to invest. Once the account is ready, you can initiate a trade.

When you trade in a brokerage account, you will be offered choices about how the trade should be placed. The most common trade is a *limit order*. The investor puts in a maximum price that he is willing to pay for the ETF and the ETF is not bought unless it gets down to that price or below. This means that the trade may not happen if the price does not go down to or below your limit price. The buyer can also allow the limit order to expire at the end of the day or to continue until it is canceled or a number of days (usually 60) has passed. The investor needs to be careful when using Good Till Canceled since they are easy to forget and may make a trade when market conditions have changed so that you no longer wish to buy that ETF.

The buyer also has the choice of a market order which means that the ETF will be bought at the next available price. This is rarely a good idea, especially when the ETF or stock is thinly traded. Opportunistic traders can take advantage of a market order to sell you an ETF at a premium.

High Dividend ETFs

You first investment in an All-weather Market is a high dividend ETF.

A dividend is a portion of the company's profit that is paid to the shareholders. Over half of U.S. publicly traded companies pay some kind of dividend. It is usually only a fraction, but it can be more than the company's entire profit because the company is trying to maintain an established track record of paying dividends. Dividends are usually paid in cash, although they can be in shares in the company. The company can choose their own time frame for paying dividends, but they are usually paid quarterly, although it is not unusual to see special one-time dividends paid near the end of the year, usually for tax reasons.

High-yield means that the dividends are greater than the average dividend of the S&P 500, which is currently about 1.85%. A high yield often reflects a company's mature status. Since the business has relatively few profitable growth investments it can pursue, it returns most of its cash flow to shareholders in the form of dividends. Utilities, telecom, energy, financial, materials and health companies tend to pay dividends. Companies that are still growing and developing, such as technology or pharmaceutical companies, usually don't pay dividends since they feel that the best use of their profit is to re-invest in the company's growth. Because dividend companies are generally stable and mature, they tend to be less volatile than non-dividend stocks, and tend to decline less in recessions and crashes.

Some retired investors like to use dividends as a cash flow to live on. That way, they never have to touch their capital. This is a good idea if you want to make your undeserving brats fabulously wealthy when you die. Otherwise, treat your dividends just like any other cash, to be re-invested, kept in cash or spent according to your overall investment plan. The amount of dividends you get should have nothing to do with how much you withdraw.

Dividends are more tax efficient than ordinary income from a job, income from a pension, or withdrawing from a traditional IRA. Most dividends are "qualified," which means that they are taxed at a lower rate and are currently tax free for those in the less than 15% tax bracket. However, they are not as tax efficient as capital gains, because you have no control over when you receive them. Therefore, you must keep an eye on the amount of dividends that you are receiving to make sure that they don't disrupt you tax planning.

There are a number of ETFs that focus on high-dividend stocks such as Vanguard High Dividend Yield (VYM), Fidelity High Dividend (FDVV) and ProShares S&P 500 Dividend Aristocrats (NOBL).

25% of the money that you have invested in an All-weather Market should be in a High Dividend ETF.

Sector Momentum Trends

Companies are grouped into sectors with other similar companies. For example, Marathon Oil, Halliburton and Conoco Phillips are all in the Energy sector. This can be further divided into Industries. Marathon Oil and Conoco Phillips are both in the Oil, Gas & Consumable Fuels industry, while Haliburton is in the Energy Equipment & Services Industry. Stocks in the same Industry usually move up or down together. Sectors also move up and down together although they are more diverse.

There are ETFs that target a particular sector. I will list them with their Fidelity ETFs, although there are other good investment companies with sector ETFs. There are eleven sectors: Communication Services (FCOM), Consumer Discretionary (FDIS), Consumer Staples (FSTA), Energy (FENY), Financials (FNCL), Health Care (FHLC), Industrials (FIDU), Information Technology (FTEC), Materials (FMAT), Real Estate (FREL) and Utilities (UTIL).

In an All-weather Market, we want to look at defensive stocks that will go down less in a downturn. These are Health Care, Consumer Staples, Utilities, and Real Estate (REITs).

Create a chart in a charting website. I like PerfChart on StockCharts.com (they try to get you to buy access, but look around the website for the free charts) because it incorporates both the stock's price and its dividends to give a total return. Most other charting websites only show the price. Put in the ETFs for Consumer Staples, Health Care, Utilities and Real Estate (REITs) so that you can see the trend lines since the start of the All-weather Market period. We are going to compare their Momentum Trends.

Momentum is the tendency of an investment to persist in its trend. If it's going up, it tends to continue to go up, and if it's going down, it goes lower. A momentum strategy tries to take advantage of this tendency in the market. The strategy does not depend on looking at fundamentals or developing your own prediction of what the market will do. You cannot anticipate a trend; you can only identify one. You won't catch the first move higher; you will only jump on board after the train has left the station.

Momentum is sometimes referred to as a factor. There have been a number of factors identified that are supposed to identify market anomalies so that the investor can take advantage of them. Some of the better-known factors are small size, high quality, low volatility and hundreds of others that are less known. Studies have shown that the market does not correctly price the stocks with the factors and suggests that those in the know can take advantage of this.

Unfortunately, these factors tend to disappear once the anomaly is known. For example, after a study has shown that the market underprices low-volatility stocks, investors are willing to pay more for them. The only factor that hasn't disappeared after the anomaly is revealed is momentum. In fact, momentum appears to have increased. If you think about it for a minute, you'll understand why. If people start paying a higher price for low-volatility stocks, then the anomaly disappears and future earnings will be right in line with the price paid. However, if people start to pay higher prices for stocks with momentum, the momentum will increase and push the price even higher. Of course, eventually the price will come back to reality, but meantime the anomaly increases and a momentum strategy pays off handsomely.

Examine the chart you've created that shows the trend of your sectors since the start of the All-weather Market period. You want to invest about **10%** in whichever is doing best of Consumer Staples, Health Care, Utilities and Real Estate. Check your sectors every week while an All-weather Market continues and make adjustments to suit the trends, looking not at the immediate past, but at the trend since the start of the All-weather Market.

Bonds

An All-weather Market could go up or down, a little or a lot. The best protection against the market going down a lot are U.S. Treasury bonds. Whatever your criticism of the U.S. government and its debt, buyers of bonds know that the U.S. is the safest guarantor in the world. Neither cash, nor gold, not bitcoins come close to matching the diversifying power of bonds backed by the full faith of the U.S. government.

U.S. bonds usually have one of the lowest yields of any investment, but the importance of bonds is not their yield, but their safety. When equities and other growth investments are plunging, Treasury bonds are rising. When everyone is fleeing to safety, the safety they flee to are U.S. bonds.

Of course, there are many kinds of bonds, but Treasuries are the most defensive since they will move opposite of everything else that you'll invest in. If the market crashes, you will be able to sell your bonds at a profit and then invest them at the bottom and so regain the lion's share of your wealth during the fast upsurge that follows a crash.

Corporate Bonds will pay higher yield than treasuries, but they will provide little protection since they tend to go down when the market goes down. This is especially true of the higher yielding corporate bonds, often called junk bonds. When Treasury yields are down, the average asshole investor will "chase returns" and buy junk bonds to get the higher return that he feels is necessary. This is never a good idea, but especially not in this market. In this Early Up Market, people tend to take on too much risk for too little return, and this is exactly what buying junk bonds does. Junk bonds are priced off of Treasuries. When Treasury yields are down, so are junk bond yields. That means that you are getting less reward for more risk. The successful investor is always looking for more reward for less risk.

You can buy U.S. Treasury bonds directly online at TreasureyDirect.gov. But it is generally easier to buy them as part of an ETF. ETFs are term diversified and usually more liquid being tradable anytime the stock market is open.

When you buy a bond, you are lending money to the bond seller. The seller might be a corporation, a city, the U.S or a foreign government. Most bonds incur three risks: 1) the borrower declares bankruptcy and you don't get paid back; 2) the borrower pays you off early and so you don't receive all the expected income; and 3) you want to sell the bond early and you can't get what you paid for it. None of these risks are believed to apply to U.S. treasuries.

However, there is a fourth risk that applies to every loan. It is inflation. This means that you'll get the money that you loaned back, but that amount of money won't be worth as much. When looking at the yield of a bond, you should also figure in inflation. Yield without inflation is called a nominal return. Yield with inflation is a *real* return.

To protect yourself from whatever inflation will do, you should buy two kinds of Treasury bonds. One half of your investment should be in regular Treasuries. If inflation is less than expected regular Treasury bonds do well. However, if inflation is greater than expected, you will want to be in Treasury Inflation-Protected Securities, commonly called TIPS. These are a form of U.S. Treasury bond designed to protect investors against inflation. They are indexed to inflation and pay investors a fixed interest rate as the bond's principle value adjusts with the inflation rate

20% of your investment should be in long-term Treasury ETF, since those will give you the most protection. Vanguard's Long-Term Treasury Index Fund ETF (VGLT), SPDR Long Term Treasury ETF (SPTL) and Schwab Long-term US Treasury ETF (SCHQ) all have very low expense ratios.

20% of your money should be invested in a TIPS ETF, such as iShares TIPS Bond ETF (TIP), Schwab US TIPS ETF (SCHP).

Commodities

Commodities are the raw materials that are either consumed or used to build other products. They are a crucial part of the supply chain for almost every company and a key part of the global economy. They fall into four broad categories: metals (gold, silver, aluminum, copper), energy (oil, natural gas, heating oil), agriculture (soybeans, corn, wheat, oranges, sugar, cotton, and lumber), and livestock and meats (cattle, hogs, pork bellies). The market treats all commodities as interchangeable. Investors don't care where or when the gold was produced, or what farm the hogs are from. For the commodities market, gold is gold and pork bellies are pork bellies.

Investing in commodities is different from investing in stocks. With stocks, you own a piece of the business. You profit from its growth and lose if it goes bankrupt. Commodities neither grow nor declare bankruptcy. Instead their value goes up or down according to global demand, global production and speculation. For example, if the production of natural gas increases because of a new technology, the price of the commodity goes down. Conversely, if the demand for natural gas goes up because of a harsh winter, the price will also go up.

Commodities tend to run on their own cycles. If there's a big soybean harvest, the price goes down. Unrest in the Middle-east and the price of oil goes up. A hard winter in Florida and oranges are worth more. In addition, there is a great deal of speculation causing prices to rise or fall with the latest rumors. Also, since commodities are traded globally, fluctuations in currencies can have a large effect on their price. Because of all these factors, commodities are more volatile than most stocks or bonds. However, they are also uncorrelated with market, which makes them a good hedge when you don't know what the market is going to do.

Another reason that commodities make a good hedge against the market is that they do well during periods of high inflation. As wages increase and prices rise, so do the value of commodities.

15% of your investment in an All-weather Market should be in a commodity ETF such as PowerShares DB Commodity (DBC) or iPath Bloomberg Commodity Index Total Return ETN (DJP).

Cash

We've been told that "Cash is King," and there's a reason for that. When we are unsure of what the market is going to do, cash is the ultimate hedge. Inflation is the only threat to cash, but that is a slow erosion over time. You don't want to leave money in cash over the long run, but in periods of uncertainty, cash is your best security.

When investors say cash, they don't just mean actual dollar bills. Cash includes money-market funds, cash-management accounts maintained by brokers and short-term Treasuries. The important features are that these have very low volatility and are liquid, i.e. you can get your money out within a day or less.

The most convenient place for the investor to keep cash is in a broker's cash-managed account. These are usually swept every night into FDIC insured bank accounts and they often pay competitive interest rates. However, you must check to be sure that this is true, since some brokers depend on convenience alone to attract your money.

Money market funds and money market accounts are tied to short-term fixed income investments like U.S. Treasuries. They usually pay a bit more than savings accounts and broker cash-managed accounts. Money market *funds* are not FDIC insured against losses, but money market *accounts* are.

Short-term treasuries usually pay a little more than money-markets but they are a bit more volatile and not quite as liquid because you must wait for a buyer before you can access the money. Normally that is not a problem, but it could become a problem during times of extreme stress when you most need to pull the money out.

You should put your money into your broker's cash-management funds that pay competitive interest rates and are insured, such as Vanguard Federal Money Market or Fidelity Money Market Fund. If your broker doesn't automatically put your uninvested cash into a Money Market account. Find out how that can be arranged.

10% of your investment in an All-weather Market should be in cash.

Rebalancing

As time passes, the vagaries of the market will change your investment allocations. If bonds do really well, they may soon make up more than 8% of your investments. Rebalancing means selling and buying investments to bring you back to your original allocations. This means that you are buying those investments that performed the worst and selling those that performed the best. This may feel anti-intuitive, but research has proven this to be the best strategy. It sounds better if you say that you are buying low and selling high.

In an **All-weather Market**, your investments should look like this:

25% in a **High-dividend ETF**
10% in a **Consumer Staples, Health Care, Real Estate or Utilities Sector ETF**
20% in a **Long Treasuries ETF**
20% in a **TIPS ETF**
15% in a **Commodities ETF**
10% in **Cash**

Part Three: Cheating, Murder & Getting the Hell Out

14: Getting Your Hands Dirty: Cheating and Murder

You worked hard your whole life. You saved for retirement. You've learned how to invest it and to protect your wealth in every legitimate way. Now it's time to learn about the illegitimate ways. As my dear departed father used to say, "Sometimes you just gotta get your hands dirty."

I don't know if the world has changed since I was a kid, or if I just woke up to what was always there. But anybody who still has scruples about cheating just hasn't been paying any attention to the world today. Everybody is cheating in practically everything, from business to politics to sports to education to art and literature. How do you make millions of dollars? How do you win the Tour de France? How do you get into an Ivy-league college? How do you write a best-selling novel? You cheat. Everybody is cheating and if you don't you're at a terrible disadvantage. And in a dog-eat-dog, shark-ridden, snake-infested world, such as ours, you don't want to have a disadvantage if you can help it. Because in the end, this book is about winning at your retirement and I'm here to tell you that today you have to cheat to win.

As it happened, I had great experience in cheating. I had cheated my way through school; cheated my way through my career and cheated my way through my marriage. After a lifetime of cheating, you pick up some valuable skills, such as the ability to identify weaknesses, and the courage to take advantage of them. When I got on Wall Street, I was well prepared.

Today, everywhere is like Wall Street in the 80s. Everybody has their eye on the bottom line. And they don't mind a little cheating. In fact, everyone assumes that you'll cheat. They expect you to cheat. So why not do it?

Don't just think of yourself. Think of your children. Do you want to leave them with an example of losing or winning? Don't you want to prepare them for life in the new morality which says that cheating is the easiest way to get what you want? Life today is easier without those outmoded ideas of morality. That old morality is for pussies. My advice to you is don't be a pussy.

Insider Trading

Insider trading is when you buy or sell stocks based on confidential information that most people don't have access to. For example, if you hear from a friend who works in the Defense department that Boeing is about to get a large government contract and you buy stock in Boeing, you are doing insider trading. Technically, insider trading is illegal. Every once in a while, some ambitious DA trying to look tough on Wall Street corruption will prosecute it (e.g. James Comey's prosecution of Martha Stewart), but it is rarely applied to ordinary investors.

Everyone knows that President Trump and his cronies have made millions on insider trading. They, of course, have access to hundreds of sources of insider information, such as whether a drug will be approved by the FDA, whether a company is about to be charged by the SEC or whether the Federal Reserve will raise or lower interest rates. Members of Congress also have access to multiple sources of insider information and they have made themselves exempt from the ban on insider trading. You probably only have one or two insider sources. You would be a fool not to take advantage of any insider information you have access to.

Many economists and legal experts have argued that insider trading is actually good for the stock market. After all, the price of a stock should reflect all the available information. When insider trading is banned, the price will only reflect the publicly available information making the market less efficient. As Nobel prize winner Milton Friedman put it, "You want more insider trading, not less. You want to give the people most likely to have knowledge about deficiencies of the company an incentive to make the public aware of that." Of course, this concern about the efficiency of the market is all hogwash. Insider trading is just one more way for the rich and powerful to get richer and more powerful. Doing whatever insider trading you can will help to balance the scales a little.

Offshore Accounts

Research has shown that about 10% of the world's wealth is held in offshore accounts, some of this is illicit corporate money, but most are wealthy individuals who are avoiding income taxes, circumventing inheritance laws and protecting themselves from lawsuits. Usually offshore accounts are combined with irrevocable trusts for added protection. For example, when Mitt Romney revealed his tax returns before his run for president, we found out that he kept millions in a Swiss bank account in a trust in his wife's name.

Today, Swiss bank accounts are rarely used, since they have become widely known as a way to avoid taxes and to hide illegal income. I would recommend that you use the Isle of Man instead. For those who flunked geography, the Isle of Man is a British Dependency that sits between Northern Ireland and England. There you will find hundreds of people who will be glad to serve on the board of fake shell companies, for a small fee. This is a completely legal way to hide the identity of those who really own the money. Technically, you should submit a **Report of Foreign Bank and Financial Accounts (FBAR) with your taxes, but millions of Americans have put money into offshore accounts and neglected to file the paperwork.**

The important thing is to establish the account well before you need it. Do it before the IRS is auditing you, before you divorce your wife, before your creditors file lawsuits against you. If you wait, they will be able to easily trace recent money movements.

Taxes

Of course, you already cheat on your taxes. Everybody does, from our President on down. You inflate the value of items you donate to Goodwill. You don't report the bribes and payola that you get at work. You pay your nanny or housekeeper in cash, so that you don't have to cover part of their Social Security and Medicare taxes. But these are all small time compared to what you could save by setting up your own small business.

When you hear about corporate tax evasion, most people think about multi-national conglomerates. Of course, they do their fair share of evading, but according to the IRS, the biggest source of tax evasion are small businesses. The IRS estimates that they lose half a trillion in tax evasion by small businesses. Half a trillion! Shouldn't you get your fair share of that?

When you establish your own small business, the number of deductions multiply. You can count part of your house as your home office and deduct part of your utilities and rent. You can count your car and its gas and repairs as a business expense. If your small business is rental property, you can count most improvements to your own house as business deductions. If you are creative, having your own small business means never paying income taxes again. After all, the IRS has been so underfunded that they will only pursue cases where they can recoup millions. They don't have the manpower to go after the ordinary tax cheats. This is one place where the ordinary taxpayer has an advantage over the big guys.

Cheating on Your Wife

If you watch TV or go to the movies, you'd think that every man cheats on his wife. I, myself, have never enjoyed sex with strange women that much. I kind of like it when we know each other's turn-ons & turn-offs, even if it is a little more boring. When I've found myself up to my balls in a woman whose name I can't remember, I usually fantasize that it's Stiffany. How boring is that? The only reason that I've ever cheated was for revenge. I just wanted, somehow, to get even with my wife.

Stiffany had an unusual sexual preference. She liked to masturbate strange men. She'd be out shopping in a high-class department store, see a man looking at suits and the next thing you know, they'd be in the dressing room or behind a clothes rack, him with an astonished smile, her hand going back-and-forth like a piston.

She didn't think it was cheating. After all, no man was ever inside her. Who did she hurt? She was just playing out an innocent adolescent fantasy. After all, how is a woman to measure her success except by her ability to live out every adolescent fantasy? Some women buy a pony or an impossibly huge house. Others jerk off men in department stores, parking lots, elevators or wherever the occasion arises. I know that she had handled most of the men that I'd worked with. She liked to tell me about it. It was all part of the thrill for her, telling me the shape of their cock, the bend of their shaft, their face when they came.

It's strange, while she was giving free handjobs to every Tom's Dick is Hairy, her attitude with me was very transactional. If she got something she wanted, I would get something that I wanted. I didn't mind that so much. After all, trades like that are what I do for a living. The only problem was that she thought her vagina was worth infinitely more than my cock.

"My pussy is sacred," she said. "While your junk is just that, junk." If a trade was going to happen, it had to be my cock and a diamond broach for her vagina.

She had a point. Our entire culture seems to treat our respective genitals that way, so who am I to swim against the tide? But even when I ponied up and paid for the sex with little presents, I couldn't really enjoy it. Wherever she touched me, I could feel another cock in her hand. Another man's cock pressing against my chest and caressing my face. Their hard cocks made mine go limp. Stiffany would walk away in disgust leaving me to lie in bed, my desire and my anger smoldering.

How I Got Away with Murder

Everybody considers murdering their spouse at one time or another. The first advice that I would give a potential wife murderer is, DON'T DO IT. Because odds are you'll be caught. They always suspect the husband-- mostly because the husband is usually guilty. Don't you watch the nightly news? It's almost always the husband.

A lot of husbands will do it without planning, just winging it. They're drunk and angry and tired of being nagged. They've had it up to here and they just do it. Then they leave a nice trail for the police, doing internet searches on how to dispose of the body. Or they'll leave a blood spray on the carpet. Or they put the murder weapon in their own trash. And then when the police question them, they talk about how much they love their wife and how they wouldn't want to live without her and how they might have said once or twice that they wish she were dead, but they never really meant it.

The police handle hundreds of these cases every year, so they have a lot of experience. The husband only has the one try and it usually doesn't go well.

I had worked out an elaborate plan to murder my wife. Well, maybe plan isn't the right word, let's say fantasies. I imagined a sudden kidnapping and murder. I imagined running her over with the car. I imagined elevators failing, anvil's falling, a shove off a cliff or a subway platform. But most often I imagined reaching into my nightstand, getting my Glock and splattering her brains on the wall. It's just the sort of image that comes up when it's late at night and you're trying to sleep and she won't shut up about everything you've ever done wrong in your life.

I knew that our relationship was toxic. We were poison together. I wanted to leave but she was prone to physical violence, quick as a cat and she had the reach on me. Neither of us were happy. She certainly wasn't. All I ever heard about was how unhappy she was. Sometimes I felt like grabbing her by the shoulders and shaking. "Be happy, you crazy bitch," I wanted to scream.

At the start, she was fascinated by everything about me. After our marriage, that fascination was turned off as if by a light switch. By the end, all I wanted from her was a little respect. But to her, I was nothing. Nothings don't deserve respect, or courtesy. You don't have to play fair with nothings. You don't have to consider their feelings. Or their well-being. Or their pain.

One hot night in August 2018, I became convinced that she was planning on murdering me. She'd not been able to meet my eyes for a week. She'd avoided my touch when we had passed in the hall. When I was home for dinner, she'd eat alone in her room. Last night, to test her, I offered an emerald bracelet for sex. She took it and we had the usual professional sex, but I could not shake the feeling that she was planning to kill me. I knew that I was going to have to kill her first.

All that night, I prepared myself to kill her. I had to get my hands dirty and get the job done. I had to let go of any feelings that I had toward a fellow human being. I had to discard my instincts to love and protect. I had to be cold, hard, unrelenting.

I was afraid and angry. My feelings and emotions rattled around my skull like pennies in a clothes-dryer. My memories were in there, too. They rattled and clanked, "This isn't right. Don't do it." But I couldn't listen to them. I had to stay afraid and angry and let my rage do its work.

As I heard her pacing back and forth in her room, my rage increased. I thought that I could hear her heart pound and her blood rush. I knew that I could hear my own. But I wouldn't let my rage consume me. I just wanted to be aware of it and use it. This rage has always been in me. It has patiently waited for me to tap into it. It just wants to be there for me when I need it—when I need it to do dirty deeds. I will relax and let my rage do its work. I will be safe and calm knowing that the morning will come and the worst will soon be over. There is nothing that "I" actually need do. The rage will do it for me.

She came down to join me for breakfast as I read the Sunday paper. I knew she hadn't slept all night. Her eyes were bloodshot and puffy. Her jaw was tightly clenched.

Without looking at me, she took my cup saying, "I'll get you more coffee." I heard her breathing heavily and a spoon rattled against a cup as she took a long time to prepare my coffee.

She set the coffee in front of me, still evading my eyes, and took the chair across from me with her own cup of coffee.

"Some mornings, you just don't want to go on living," she said flatly.

I grunted non-committedly.

"Don't you sometimes just wish you could fly up to heaven? Don't you think that would really be the best?" she asked.

"I don't believe in heaven," I said without looking up from the paper.

"But I do," she said.

"Then you fly up there."

She prattled on about how God loves us and that the angels will surround us and we must accept the inevitable and resistance is futile. But I quit listening.

"Doesn't it look like a man is floating right outside our window?" I asked suddenly pointing behind her. When she turned around, I switched our cups.

I slowly drank my coffee and scrunched up my nose like I was tasting something bitter. She kept her eyes on me as she picked up her own cup and drank. She was still watching me with cold curiosity when the poison began to take effect.

A sudden violent sickness reddened her face. She froze, afraid to speak or move lest she vomit. She clutched at an icy cold gathering in her stomach and her teeth began to chatter.

"What did you say?" I asked.

"Tricked," she gasped and a yellow vomit erupted from her mouth. Her shoulders heaved and her hands clasped and unclasped in agony as she kept on retching. The room filled with her stench.

As a yellow foam dripped from her mouth, she began to softly moan. Drops of sweat oozed from her mottled face. Her dilated eyes stared at me, but I had no idea what she was actually seeing. It might have been the drapes or the wallpaper that were filling her with such fear and disgust.

She tried to get up, but a sharp gasp, like a balloon being punctured, burst from her and she was overcome with convulsions as she fell back into the chair. She slumped forward, groaning more and more loudly until a fierce twitching seized her and she fell to the floor.

She began to cough up blood. Her limbs convulsed. Her skin burned a fiery red and she scratched at her arms leaving deep gouges with her painted nails.

She screamed. She shrieked. She cursed. She implored the poison to be quick. She put her face into the deep-plush of the carpet and cried until she began to vomit again.

I don't know how long her agony went on. Hours? Again and again, she begged me to kill her. I couldn't take it anymore. I went into the bedroom and got the Glock. Just as I was about to shoot her, a one-armed man burst into the room. As my lawyer described it at the trial. "That man took the gun from the defendant. That man shot and killed her. That man fled the scene, and the police are said to be close to his arrest any minute." My lawyer and I still have a million-dollar bounty for whomever will bring him to justice.

As you already know, the jury acquitted me. It's better to be rich than innocent.

15: Retiring Abroad

After I was acquitted, the fake media had it in for me. I was constantly hounded by reporters who would ask the most asinine questions, like "Did you do it?" What did they expect me to say, "Of course I did!"? It was the same thing that they did to OJ, to Diana, to Tyson and to the many other completely innocent people who have been hounded by the fake media.

As usual, they claimed that I was racist, misogynist and worse. You kill one woman and suddenly you're a misogynist. Here's a report on my so-called "racism" by the Times:

When asked about the race of the one-armed man, Robbins said, "How should I know?" When asked if the one-armed man was African-American, Robbins said, "Is Meghan Markel African-American? Is Halle Berry? Is Bill Clinton? I don't want to express an opinion on anybody's race."

So you see, not having an opinion these days is racist. That's just the way that 'those people' are, those god-damned lamestream reporters.

I knew that I had to get out of the US and soon. But to get back to the subject of this book, *Getting and Staying Rich in Retirement*, there are many economic and demographic reasons that every retired baby-boomer should think about getting out. It's not only for those who have just been acquitted of murdering their wife.

Consider where a broke and in-debt nation is going to get their money when the deficit-spending express explodes in a fiery crash. All of that money that you have squirreled away in government-tracked IRAs and federally-regulated brokerages is going to look mighty tantalizing.

Also consider what the flood of aging baby-boomers is going to do to the health-care system. What will senior care cost when everybody is old, young Americans want "fulfilling" jobs and we're keeping out cheap immigrant labor? What will medical care be like after bickering partisanship has ruined ObamaCare, bankrupt Medicaid and given us Medicare for None? What will happen to all of the poor elderly who have lost their pension or whose retirement savings consisted of buying a lottery ticket every week? Will they just be left to starve on our corners or beg on our streets? Personally, if I'm going to live in a country full of starving beggars, I rather that it be strangers instead of my former neighbors.

Choosing Your New Home

Whether you're a liberal dismayed by Trump, a conservative worried by the deficit, a person of color frightened by the implacable racism, a Christian afraid that the ACLU will take away your Church, a gun owner who's afraid they'll take away your gun, or an innocent wife-murderer. You'll want to ask yourself "How do I get out?" And you might want to ask that soon to avoid the rush.

Whatever your motive for getting out, living in another country is an opportunity to enhance your life and, if you so desire, to reinvent yourself. It's a big, interesting world out there and many retirees relocate just to satisfy their wanderlust and curiosity. Others want an affordable cost of living, lower tax bill, warmer weather and a healthier lifestyle. Choosing another country to live in is a lot like choosing a spouse. Nobody else can tell you what will make you happy. Some people prefer a bustling city, others a quiet beach. Everybody has a different list of desires and different tolerances. The best you can do is to know the right questions and go on a few dates.

Actually, to say that you are choosing a country is a rough approximation. When you evaluate where you live right now, you probably aren't thinking in terms of the United States, but of the region, city, neighborhood and even house that you live in. You'll want to think of your retirement location in the same way. You aren't going to retire to France or Uruguay. You're going to retire to a small apartment in the middle of Paris or a seaside villa in La Barra.

Probably the best way to approach your choice is to try to imagine what a typical day would be like. When you wake up in the morning and look out the window, would you see a pristine beach stretching off into the horizon? As you sit on the veranda drinking coffee, would you look down into a bustling crowd of fashionable men and sophisticated women on their way to work? When you stroll out to do some shopping, would you select from dock-fresh fish, exotic fruits and a mishmash of hawkers? Try to imagine it all the way through to a last look out your bedroom window when you turn out the lights.

Your choice and its cost will depend a lot on how much you want it to be like the United States. First of all, it must be said that, for better or for worse, no place is just like the United States, but if you are willing to spend the money and limit your choices, you can probably find something pretty close. For example, if you move to Panama and buy everything from the local Walmart, make friends only with your fellow expats and subscribe to American cable TV, your life will not be that different. In fact, I would say that in certain Panamanian expat enclaves, you will see so many fat-assed, hair-dyed, pale-skinned Americans that you'll think you're back in Iowa.

On the other hand, for less money, every trip to the store could be a new adventure, everybody you meet an amiable expert on their culture, and you could have plenty of time to reflect on the day's events and what they mean in the greater scheme of things.

In choosing a new country to live in, you should ask the following six pairs of questions. In each case, the first question is about you and the second about the place.

1. Do you want to learn a new language? Is the local language difficult to learn?

If English isn't the native language, then not learning the local language will restrict your involvement and limit your understanding of your everyday world. You will have to listen to what seems like gibberish when you walk about the streets and stroll through the parks. If you get a letter from the electric company, you will have to ask someone to read it to you. You will have to rely on the forbearance of strangers for many simple interactions. You will miss some of the nuance of those who are haltingly translating their thoughts into English.

However, learning a new language is not easy for everyone and some languages are particularly difficult, especially when the language embodies an alien culture with its own set of unexamined assumptions and traditions. For some people, just having to remember which noun is masculine and which is feminine is too much trouble.

2. Is justice and equality for all a crucial value? How oppressive is the local government?

Every human institution has some corruption and inequality, so you probably already know what your tolerance is for it. Are you somebody who fumes and fulminates over every small injustice or can you shrug your shoulders and hope that someday karma will even things out?

If you think a trip to the DMV is unbearable, wait until you experience a bureaucracy that handles everything differently, from how to fill out the initial form, to how to communicate a final decision. You will run into many offices that you cannot understand, and never will, and wouldn't really want to. Would you be able to see these as an interesting anthropological case or would you blow your top?

Some countries are run by criminals masquerading as statesmen. These countries are usually ones that you would not want to live in for other reasons such as frequent strikes, fuel shortages, social strife, currency crises and power blackouts. But such governments usually have a tightly limited scope for power and are easily bribed, so you may be able to find a wonderful corner where you are left alone so long as you don't try to organize the workers or protest environmental threats.

You can go to www.freedomhouse.org for a rating on different countries. They look at human rights, the justice system, inequality, a free press and internet and boil it down to a rating of free, partly free and not free. In case you're wondering, the U.S. is still ranked as free.

3. Do you need all the infrastructure of modern life? What necessities are easily available in the community?

We all feel like we need hi-speed internet. I certainly feel that way, but I also remember a hit song that proclaimed, "I want my MTV" and nobody wants that anymore. Do you really need drinkable water every time you turn the tap? Do you need concrete highways? How many times a week do you really need your mail delivered? Does every little town need a sewage system? Your answer to such mundane questions may determine your list of possible relocations.

Don't make any assumptions about the particular locality. There are some parts of the world that completely skipped over the landline and went straight to cell phones, who never had any luck with brick-and-mortar banks but are thriving with online ones. Consequently, there are many poor countries where hi-tech infrastructure is easily available, at least in certain communities. You have to do your homework. Because infrastructure is important to global capitalism, it is easy to find up-to-date information on it. Go to the World Bank webpage (econ.worldbank.org), the World Economic Forum (www.weforum.com), or the CIA World Factbook (www.cia.gov).

4. Could you stand to live in a country with frequent mass murders, scores of serial killers, and random drive-by shootings? Do you live in such a country now?

Outside of a war zone or other massive turmoil, there are few places in the world with as much deadly crime as there is in the U.S. When you leave the U.S., your risk of getting shot, raped or mugged goes down. However, your risk of getting burglarized, cheated or pickpocketed goes up. In many parts of the world, rich Americans with expensive laptops and brand-name shoes are seen as legitimate prey. And if you leave any valuable item vulnerable to a smash-and-run, you have just made a donation to the local boys club.

As with the US, the particular locality is more important than national statistics. Your best source of local crime information are expats who live there. Do a Google search on "expat group" and the name of the country you are considering. Most expats are happy to let you know the local problems.

5. What is the state of your health and do you have a particular pre-existing condition? How available is top-notch, affordable health care in the community?

Most places that you would consider retiring to will have more affordable health care than the U.S. All the developed world and much of the undeveloped world have comprehensive national health plans available to both citizens and residents. However, the rules for non-citizen residents are peculiar to each country and must be investigated for your particular choice. In addition, the availability of specialists and top-notch hospitals will usually depend on the locality. The choices for health care in a major city are going to be different from those in a rural outpost. Again, a local expat can help with that information.

If you have a pre-existing condition, that will be your first concern. You will want to know that the specialists for your specific condition are available in the country. A pre-existing condition may also affect your eligibility for a national health plan, so that needs to be investigated.

The biggest problem that retirees with health problems face is that Medicare is not accepted outside the U.S. However, even with the loss of Medicare, health care in most countries is still comparatively cheaper. Some people prefer a country that is close enough that they can return to the U.S. for Medicare services. That way they get the best of both worlds.

6. How often will you want to return to the U.S.? How difficult is it to get back from the community?

Most countries have flights to the U.S., many of them direct. However, multiple trips a year can quickly add up to your biggest retirement expense.

Some people only plan on living in the new country part time and to make one back and forth trip a year to follow the weather. Others may have family obligations, health problems or unfinished business that will require them to travel back often. These costs need to be put into your budget. Again, the cost and convenience depends upon where you live in the country. If you are going back often, you will want to live close to an international airport and you might want to limit your consideration to places that are less than a one-day flight away.

Get the Hell Out

A week after my acquittal, two police detectives rang my doorbell. Freedmon and Laurence. I knew them well from the investigation into my wife's murder. "What do you boys want?" I asked through the intercom. I liked to call them "boy" because they're both Black as the ace of spades and it kind of pisses them off.

"We'd like to come in," Freedmon said.

"Do you have a warrant?" I asked.

"We just want to talk."

"Go ahead and talk, I can hear you fine through the intercom."

"We just want to clear a few things up."

"Go right ahead. Speak clearly into the intercom."

"So you're not going to let us in."

"Of course, I'll let you in with a warrant. Why don't you boys just run out to a judge, let's say Judge Nalipino, and get a warrant. I'll wait."

"You know Nalipino is not going to give us a warrant."

"I know. I know. The problems of bureaucracy are everywhere. I totally sympathize with your frustrations, but you know, that's your problem, not mine."

"Look, I can make up a reasonable suspicion and break the fucking door down."

"Go right ahead. After the last time you got caught making one up, who knows? Maybe they'll be more lenient the second time. You should know, however, that I have cameras everywhere that transmit to a remote location. You wouldn't want to say or do anything that a judge might find questionable. Or, Oh my goodness, you already did."

Suddenly there was a loud bang, followed by a yell as though someone had hit a metal-plated door with their fist and broken a finger.

Needless to say, they didn't come back with a warrant, but I knew that I had to disappear. I thought that it was mainly the Press, but they clearly had some cops in their pocket, so they would have access to any sources the police would have access to that didn't require a warrant. And of course, those warrant rules could always be bent, folded, spindled and mutilated.

But my greatest fear was Kate, Stiffany's best friend who had worked for Hillary Clinton, so she knew how to make people disappear. She had the money to pursue me to the ends of the earth and the connections who would do things that might not be exactly legal. Despite being best friends, they never seemed that close, but you never know what might get into that rich bitch's head. She would be the greatest threat in the near future. After I'm off her radar for a while, she'll forget and move onto another petty whim.

If you want to disappear, you can't just walk out the door and vanish, like the good old days. We live in the information age and we are constantly creating information all the time. Every time you carry your phone, use your credit card, send an email, make a phone call or receive mail, you are creating information. In fact, I could fill this book with nothing but a list of sources of information that we create every day, and I would quickly run out of room. And all that information seems to last forever and much of it remains accessible, to anyone willing to pull some strings and call in some favors.

In the information age, the trick is not to disappear so much, as it is to obscure and divert. Instead of fighting the proliferation of information, I was going to use it to dismay my pursuers. I was going to create multiple false trails, each one of which would require effort and time and money to pursue. And at each dead-end they will be faced with the choice of pursuing yet another dead end. Unless you blew up a building, married royalty or ratted on the mafia, most people gave up after one or two dead ends.

The first step was to obscure, i.e. minimize the information being produced outside my control. Needless to say, I'll only give you the broad strokes and the devil is in the details. I quit using all my credit cards and my cell phone. I took out enough cash to live on for 6 months and extras for equipment and bribes. I downloaded everything on my computer and the cloud to a portable drive and quit using my computer for any real purposes. I bought prepaid credit cards, a prepaid cell phone and a new laptop computer.

The next step was to establish an escape route in case something went wrong. I bought a small motorcycle with my prepaid credit card, rented a nearby garage and put together a "Never Come Back" bag. If the shit hit the fan sooner than expected, I could sneak over to the garage and have the bare essentials I would need to get out.

I was ready to start on the divert part of my plan. All of this would be done on my old computer and my old cell phone. On my computer, I searched for real estate companies in a medium-size Midwestern town. I contacted the realtor and arranged to rent one of their apartments. I made sure that the realtor would run a credit check on me tied to that location. I then applied for utilities and phone service from that address. And I opened up a small checking account at a local bank.

Using my old cell phone. I set up a similar diversion in a Canadian city. I would repeat this with two other cities in another week.

I gave my old credit card to a trusted friend who traveled a lot and asked him to make small purchases wherever he went. Soon my credit card records were showing me buying things in Singapore, San Francisco and Tokyo.

That should be enough diversion for now.

The next step was to get out without being detected. I went to a busy coffee shop that offered unsecured wireless Internet service and I arranged to have an Uber pick me up for a trip to upstate New York. I had him drop me at a bus station in Niagara Falls. I walked around the dark corners of the bus station until I found somebody who would sell me a birth certificate and a social security card. It's easier than you think, millions of people have their identities stolen every year and false identities were just one of the ways that they made money off it.

I caught another Uber back to the city. I spent the next week establishing my new purchased identity and setting up dummy corporations in both my real name and with my new identity. I began to transfer money and other real property to separate dummy corporations, so that one corporation had my bank account, another owned my penthouse and I spread my investments around several corporate owned brokerage accounts.

I was ready to go, but I was still hoping that I might be able to take some of my possessions with me. However, Kate called and said she wanted to come over and give me something that she knew Stiffany would like to see me get. I told her to come over in an hour. I snuck out the back of my building, left all my belongings behind, got my "Never Come Back" bag and took my motorcycle to the airport.

The TSA officer at the international airport looked barely out of his teens as he quickly examined my fake id. After he had waved me through and my bags and body had been scanned, I sat outside my gate still expecting at any minute to be tackled by security guards. I knew the next big test would be immigration and customs at the destination, but I couldn't think of that now. I'd have plenty of time on the long trip to think of how I'd get through that and what I'd do after. I took a deep breath and tried to appear calm. I thought that soon I'll be in the air and can relax, but I was wrong.

After all the passengers were seated and before we pulled away from the gate, two women in dark pantsuits who identified themselves as New York City detectives came on board. They came straight toward me, but stopped in front of the man two rows ahead me.

"Mr. Turner come with us."

"Why, I didn't do anything," he whined.

"Please come with us so we can clear this thing up."

"But I didn't do anything, I swear. I'm only behind a couple of months. I don't know why they call it child support, anyway. She spends it all."

By now the detectives had him up out of his seat. One held his arms as the other put some tape over his mouth. They pulled him down the aisle as he looked imploringly from side to side, showing the whites of his eyes.

Apart from that, everything went smoothly. I went from La Guardia to London to fly to Jamaica and then took a puddlejumper to Barbados and finally from there to my current location. Under my fake name and using the techniques that I've outlined in this book, I quickly made my fortune back. I live now in paradise, surrounded by friends and scoundrels and am the happiest of my life.

There's only one thing missing. Vengeance. But that's your job. Go out and take all that money away from those fat bastards who have been taking it away from you all your life. You are my legacy and my revenge.

www.ingramcontent.com/pod-product-compliance
Lightning Source LLC
Chambersburg PA
CBHW060418220526
45465CB00008B/2935